The Oldest Revolutionary
Essays on Benjamin Franklin

Percy G. Adams

Bruce I. Granger

John Griffith

William L. Hedges

J. A. Leo Lemay

Cameron C. Nickels

David L. Parker

Lewis P. Simpson

P. M. Zall

THE OLDEST REVOLUTIONARY

Essays on Benjamin Franklin

Edited by J. A. Leo Lemay

University of Pennsylvania Press/1976

Copyright © 1976 by The University of Pennsylvania Press, Inc.
Cover portrait of Franklin from painting by C. W. Peale, courtesy of
the American Philosophical Society.
All rights reserved
Library of Congress Catalog Card Number: 75-41618
ISBN: 0-8122-7707-4
Printed in the United States of America

In memory of
THEODORE HORNBERGER (1906-1975)
Our teacher and friend

Contents

❧ Introduction

Benjamin Franklin, the oldest Revolutionary, embodied the European ideas of America at the outbreak of the American Revolution. America meant possibility, especially the possibility for the common man to become uncommon. America was the promise of a new life, a better life, a dream for the future. America promised that a man might not only become free from pressing financial worry—he might also renew his spirit and recreate himself as a new man. America held out the prospect of new possibilities for mankind, for democracy, and for the individual.

Franklin's fame as a scientist, his renown as a spokesman for democracy, his espousal of mankind, of the possibilities of life, and of America—all tended to create an image of Franklin as the representative American.

He was and he wasn't. Leaving aside the unpleasant reality of the impossibility for the mass of common men to become uncommon (the impossibility for those with little extraordinary talent and little determination—the men of no demons—to become famous), there is still Franklin's own unsuitability for the role of the representative American. In addition to his extraordinary talents, unflagging energies, great pride, and even greater ambition, we must still confront the Franklin who was not only NOT a true believer—he was most assuredly a practical, hardheaded, commonsensical realist.

His unflinching realism did not result in pessimistic, paralyzing nihilism. Instead, he advocated a Pascal-like attitude toward life and human beings and oneself. He urged skeptics and pessimists to live as if life were enjoyable, as if fellow human beings were worth-while, and as if one respected and liked oneself. For only if one went through these motions could the possibility exist for life to be good. And if one continuously lived life as if it were good, then this might finally become the fact.

In Franklin's day there was no widespread national malaise concerning America, and he was not writing primarily for skeptics and pessimists, or even for those, like himself, who had journeyed through a dark night of the soul. (When he fell extremely ill at twenty-one, he was not unhappy to die, and felt discouraged only when he began to recover and found that he would have the whole "disagreeable" prospect of life before him—but he made the most of it.) He wrote the *Autobiography* primarily for late-eighteenth-century adolescents and young adults of the Old World who were looking for standards, looking for ways to live, looking for places to live, looking for possible attitudes toward life, and looking for models. He wrote it with great art. And if we can escape our own preconceptions of Franklin as the representative American of our late-twentieth-century America, and imagine him speaking for the America of 1771, of 1784, and of 1788—when he wrote the book and when America was possibility—then we may not, perhaps, blame him quite so much for being the representative American of an America that we have created. Or if we read what Franklin actually wrote—and are blinded neither by the 1775 or the 1975 image of America nor by Franklin as (what he never was) the representative American—then we may learn something of the truth, as well as the art, of his writings. The truth includes Franklin the idealist, refusing in his mid-sixties the British overtures of a sinecure in order to cast his lot with the New World. The oldest signer of the Declaration of Independence was a man who at sixty-nine risked his comfort, fortune, and life when his peers (and his son) were retiring with what money they could take out of the colonies to the safety of England's leisure world.

The following essays deal with some of the writings and some of the activities of Franklin. Taken separately, they provide valuable insights into what Franklin was and wrote; taken together, they provide an overview of Franklin's attitudes, purposes, and significances as a writer and thinker for his own time and for ours.

L. L.

Los Angeles, California

PART I

Franklin in Action—
Printer, Press Agent, Traveler

Lewis P. Simpson   ❧ The Printer as a

Man of Letters: Franklin and the

Symbolism of the Third Realm

"I, Benjamin Franklin, of Philadelphia, printer, late Minister Plenipotentiary for the United States of America to the Court of France, and President of the State of Pennsylvania . . ."[1]

Although he had not followed the printing trade since 1748, when he had withdrawn from active participation in a printing and bookselling house to enter upon his various and widely influential public life as man of letters and statesman, Franklin recognized in his last will and testament in 1788 that the second part of his career was at one with the first. He confirmed the prophecy of his career made at the age of twenty-two, when the youthful Philadelphia printer, suffering from pleurisy, had somewhat prematurely composed his own epitaph.

The Body of
B Franklin Printer
(Like the Cover of an old Book
Its Contents torn out
And stript of its Lettering & Gilding)
Lies here, Food for Worms.
But the Work shall not be lost;
For it will, (as he believ'd) appear once more,
In a new and more elegant Edition
Revised and corrected
By the Author.

3

In this "most famous of American epitaphs,"[2] as Carl Van Doren calls it, Franklin exemplifies his ability to make homely apostrophe the ironic mask of sophisticated cultural observation. When the individual existence inevitably falls into disrepair, according to Franklin's vision of things, it will be brought out in a new and more beautiful edition by a God who, like Franklin, is not only an author but a printer. He will both correct the errata of the first edition and make the new edition typographically elegant. In Franklin's epitaph salvation by faith in the regenerating grace of God becomes faith in the grammatical and verbal skills and in the printing shop know-how of a Deity who is both Man of Letters and Master Printer.

This symbolic representation of the God of Reason is as appropriate to the Age of the Enlightenment as the more familiar symbolism depicting Him as the Great Clock Maker. In proclaiming his adherence to deism, Franklin implies his rejection of the order of existence under which he had been reared, that of the New England theocracy. He suggests an awareness of his affiliation with an order of mind and spirit which as yet existed only in tentative ways in colonial America: an order additional to the realms of Church and State—the autonomous order of mind, the Republic of Letters, or a Third Realm, being made manifest as never before in Western civilization by the advancing technology of printing. Franklin's epitaph signifies the historical engagement of his whole career with the articulation of, and the expansion and consolidation of, the Third Realm in America.

I

Although the differentiation of the Third Realm in the Western symbolization of the orders of existence is difficult to document with any degree of exactitude, three phases in the history of this process may be briefly noted. In the first we discover the remoter origins of the Third Realm in a "Second Realm" of Grecian and Roman times. This was first instituted in the Athens of Socrates, Plato, and Aristotle, where a society of philosophers made a realm apart from the integral realm of religious and political power constituting the government of the City State. Later in the Rome of Cicero and Virgil, the Second Realm was ideally constituted in two visions of intellectual and literary community: the Stoic vision of a cosmopolis of mind and the pastoral vision of Arcadia. These were the invisible homelands of spiritual elites removed from the conjoined politics and religion of the imperial state. The more immediate origins of the Third Realm are to be located in the intellectual and literary existence of the later Middle Ages. Then, as a result of the differentiation of a struggle between Church and State—a struggle, not previously known in history, between a transcendent order of Being and the temporal order of existence—a Republic of Letters emerged from the Republic of Christ. In the grand design of the medieval papacy this Third Realm would find its rationale in its function as the agency of the assimilation and harmonization of Church and State; it would, as Christopher Dawson remarks, "effect the intellectual organization of Christian civilization." The rise of the universities and the complementary efforts centering in the quest of a unified Christian Republic, however, tended in the twelfth and thirteenth centuries to place an emphasis on intellect and verbal skills that disrupted the very quest. When the papacy began to seek to elevate the Orders of Friars within the university corporations, the secular clergy of the corporations resisted. The result was a quarrel which, Dawson observes, "foreshadows the future secularization of Western culture." As the design of unity came more and more into crisis, both as a result of pressures from within the realm of the Church and of events from without, the secularization of mind was specifically, if ironically, foreshadowed in the vision of Joachim of Flora. Joachim saw "the coming of a new age, the Age of the Spirit and the Eternal Gospel in which the Church will be renewed in the liberty of the spirit under the leadership of the new order of Spiritual Contemplatives."[3] This vision of Christendom dominated by a community of spiritually perfected monks— which harks back to the Stoic vision of a community or Second Realm of sages—could be adapted to variant concepts of secular intellectual order. It offered an image of an ecumenicalism of mind opposite to that afforded by the image of the university; and, as the latter image declined in importance, it supported the rise of a dominion of humanists as the Third Realm. This is the character of the Republic of Letters as it is represented, say, by a great Renaissance scholar such as Julius Caesar Scaliger, or in a less determinate but possibly more significant way by Erasmus. But the representation of the Third Realm became more various as the secularization of thought progressed and, with the loss of Latinity and the acceptance of the vernacular modes, its languages became manifold. It came to embrace the new science as well as classical humanism— although, it is of fundamental importance to observe, all activity of mind, down through the eighteenth century, continued to be viewed under the aspect of the use of letters. And through the eighteenth century this aspect continued to be seen as comprehensive. Meanwhile, the third, and most decisive, phase in the differentiation of the Republic of Letters was inaugurated by the invention of printing in the fifteenth century. This was eventually to result in the fragmentation and diffusion of the Third

Realm; but the initial result was its expansion and growth in power. In the seventeenth and eighteenth centuries the Third Realm embraced a "classless" and crucial group of world historical men of letters: among them, Francis Bacon, Newton, Milton, Locke, Pope, Voltaire, Diderot, Hume, Franklin, John Adams, Jefferson. These intellectuals, together with numerous equal or lesser counterparts, over a period of a century and a half elaborated a comprehensive and searching inquiry into the meaning of the orders of existence. They shaped a Great Critique of Church and State.

The uniformity and repeatability of the printed word opened up the Great Critique, and the Third Realm as a whole, to the general society, creating a relationship between literacy and society never before known. Making for a more absolute distinction between literacy and illiteracy—between the man of letters and the man of no letters—the expansion of the Third Realm at the same time introduced a distinction between degrees of literacy. This obtained between the man *of* letters and the man *with* letters; between the man who practices the art of letters (the man who has a vocation to letters) and persons whose use of letters ranges from that of the "general reader" to that of the person who cannot do more than inscribe his name. Under such cultural conditions the man *of* letters could seek to extend and enhance the quality of the literacy of the man *with* letters; he could seek, up to a point at least, to democratize the dominion in which the man of letters functions. Or he could endeavor to maintain the dominion of letters as an exclusive, elitist polity of mind. In either case the nature of literacy as a dominion became a historical issue. In the first instance the liberation of the general mind through the extension of the Republic of Letters was conceived. In the second the confinement of letters and learning to the approximate scope it had achieved before the age of printing was conceived. These polar impulses were present in seventeenth- and eighteenth-century America, but Franklin's expression of them has to be understood in connection with a special differentiation of the Third Realm under the conditions of New England Puritanism.

The founding of Harvard College in 1636 embodied the Third Realm in New England. Established to perpetuate a learned ministry in the Puritan theocracy, Harvard descended from the conception of the realm of letters and learning as the servant of the autonomy of the Church. But Puritanism—and indeed the whole dissenting and reformist movement lumped under the head of Protestantism—had developed after humanism had become influential in the differentiation of the Third Realm. The New England assimilation of Church and Letters showed increasing evidences of humanistic leavening in the later seventeenth century. Moreover, the New England clergy, in common with the Puritan clergy as a whole, had originated as a learned class—an intelligentsia—alienated from an official Church and State. The Puritan clerics in England assumed the role, Michael Walzer says, "of a clerical third estate," and in this capacity "tended to anticipate the intellectual and social changes characteristic of a secular third estate."

> Their "plain-speaking" and matter-of-fact style; their insistence upon education and independent judgment; their voluntary association outside the corporate church; their emphasis upon methodical, purposive endeavor, their narrow unemotional sense of order and discipline—all this clearly suggested a life-style very different from that of a feudal lord, a Renaissance courtier or even an Anglican archbishop. This new style was first tested on the margins and in the interstices of English society by men cut off from the traditional world, angry and isolated clerics, anxiously seeking a new order. It was by no means the entirely spontaneous creation of those sturdy London merchants and country gentlemen who later became its devoted advocates; it was something they learned, or rather, it was something some of them learned. The automatic burgher values—sobriety, caution, thrift—did not constitute the significant core of Puritan morality in the seventeenth century; the clerical intellectuals had added moral activism, the ascetic style, and the quality of high-mindedness and taught these to their followers.[4]

Among the followers was John Milton, the greatest exemplar of the intelligentsia of the laity among the Puritans. In *Areopagitica,* a classic document of the effort to establish the autonomy of the Third Realm, Milton defended the "truth" of the "commonwealth of learning" and attacked the fallacy of censorship imposed in the name of religious authority. In New England the life style of the third estate of Puritanism was more circumscribed than it was in England, but a basic disposition to respect the Republic of Letters is evidenced not only in the history of Harvard but in the development of the Boston-Cambridge community as the seat of the Enlightenment in New England. By the end of the first quarter of the eighteenth century, the rise of an independent order of secular men of letters was a possibility in the Boston world. One of its first manifestations was the appearance in 1721 of the *New England Courant,* edited by Benjamin Franklin's older brother James, who had returned to Boston after completing an apprenticeship to a London printer. During his connection with this little paper Benjamin Franklin began his personal representation of the Third Realm in New England and in America.

II

Franklin's fundamental response to the Age of Printing was his discovery that it opened to the person of talent and ambition a self-education in letters and learning; his initiation into the actual techniques of the printing trade was no more than secondary to his unfolding vision of the intellectual resources of the printer's product and commodity.

The description of how he made himself into a scholar and writer is a noted passage in the *Autobiography*. Before he was twelve he began to read as chance and fortune brought books into his hands, investing whatever small sums of money he acquired in books, selling a set of Bunyan to purchase "R. Burton's historical collections," making his way through volumes of polemic divinity in his father's library when nothing else was available, reading "abundantly" in Plutarch, and eventually falling upon Defoe's *Essay on Projects* and Cotton Mather's *Essays to Do Good* (which he apparently assumed emphasized good works instead of saving grace). After he was apprenticed he secured books clandestinely from acquaintances among apprentices to Boston booksellers. ("Often I sat in my room reading the greatest part of the night, when the book was borrowed in the evening and to be returned early in the morning, lest it should be found missing or wanted.") At length a merchant, "an ingenious, sensible man, Mr. Matthew Adams," who often visited the printing house and who had "a pretty collection of books," invited the youth to make use of them. As he assiduously pursued the role of scholar, Franklin conceived the greater possibility of becoming a self-made writer. Having enjoyed some success with two Grubstreet ballads hawked about Boston only to be admonished by his father that "verse-makers were generally beggars," Benjamin turned to "prose writing" as the discipline offering the "principal means of Advancement." When he found his style "far short in elegance of expression, in method and in Perspicuity," as compared to that of his friend John Collins (with whom he had contested in a written debate), young Franklin—in an age when the fortuity of print had made history subject to the chance encounter between a mind and a book—"met with an odd volume of the *Spectator*."

> It was the third. I had never before seen any of them. I bought it, read it over and over, and was much delighted with it. I thought the writing excellent and wished if possible to imitate it. With that view, I took some of the papers, and making short hints of the sentiment in each sentence, laid them by a few days, and then without looking at the book, tried to complete the papers again by expressing each hinted sentiment at length and as fully as it had been expressed before, in any suitable words that should occur to me.[5]

Franklin's imitation of the *Spectator* became more elaborate and arduous. To force himself to seek a greater variety in his vocabulary he transformed some of Mr. Spectator's stories into verse, and subsequently when he had "pretty well forgotten the prose, turned them back again." He scrambled the organization of thoughts and topics in the original papers and then sought to restore them to wholeness. Thus he taught himself "method in the arrangement of the thoughts." Franklin was, he says, "extremely anxious" to become "a tolerable English writer."[6] But in shaping himself into an author Franklin learned something more important to success than felicity of style. He learned that in the Age of Print a successful style involves a strategy of intimacy. This strategy is important in the *Spectator,* but it may be that the precocious Franklin discerned its significance earlier through his reading of a pure exemplification of the self-taught writer in the Age of Print, John Bunyan. That this could be the case is indicated in Franklin's recollection of an incident aboard a boat when he was on his way to Philadelphia to seek his fortune.

> In crossing the bay we met with a squall that tore our rotten sails to pieces, prevented our getting into the kill, and drove us upon Long Island. On our way a drunken Dutchman who was a passenger, too, fell overboard; when he was sinking, I reached through the water to his shock pate and drew him up so that we got him in again. His ducking sobered him a little, and he went to sleep, taking first out of his pocket a book which he desired I would dry for him. It proved to be my old favourite author Bunyan's *Pilgrim's Progress* in Dutch, finely printed on good paper with copper cuts, a dress better than I had ever seen it wear in its own language. I have since found that it has been translated into most of the languages of Europe, and suppose it has been more generally read than any other book except, perhaps, the Bible. Honest John was the first that I know of who mixes narration and dialogue, a method of writing very engaging to the reader, who in the most interesting parts finds himself, as it were, admitted into the company and present at the conversation. Defoe has imitated him successfully in *Robinson Crusoe,* in his *Moll Flanders,* and other pieces; and Richardson has done the same in his *Pamela,* etc.[7]

The reader "admitted into the company, and present at the conversation." Franklin grasped one of the key motives of modern literacy: the identity of author and reader. Under an imperative of intimacy the postbardic author imitates the life of the "general reader." The author wears the guise of the reader, or, in a more intricate sense, disguises himself as the reader.

How well Franklin early comprehended the novel role of the

writer in the extension of literacy through printing is illustrated in the
Dogood Papers, which he contributed anonymously to the *New England
Courant* in 1722, being then sixteen years old. Silence Dogood—a feminine
Mr. Spectator carefully localized in manner and conversation—is a sophisticated persona; she is the youthful genius Franklin, the apprentice
"leather-apron man" (printer), masquerading as the moral identity of the
"common reader'" in the age when secular moralism began to dominate
post-theocratic New England. Silence begins her career as a writer by
acknowledging the changing role of the author: "And since it is observed,
that the Generality of People, now a days, are unwilling either to com-
mend or dispraise what they read, until they are in some measure informed who or what the Author of it is, whether he be *poor or rich, old
or young, a Schollar* or a *Leather Apron Man,* &c. and give their Opinion
of the Performance, according to the Knowledge which they have of the
Author's Circumstances, it may not be amiss to begin with a short Account of my past Life and present Condition, that the Reader may not
be at a Loss to judge whether or no my Lucubrations are worth his
reading."[8]

Born on shipboard while her parents were emigrating from
England to New England and almost at once orphaned when her father
was swept overboard by a wave while he stood on the ship's deck rejoic-
ing at her birth, Silence is the widow of a country minister to whom she
was once apprenticed. The minister had acquired a library, "which tho'
it was but small, yet it was well chose, to inform the Understanding
rightly and enable the Mind to frame great and noble Ideas"; and in this
little dominion of the mind Silence has become a student of letters. She
is, one supposes, insufficiently liberated by present-day standards to be
referred to as a "person of letters" instead of a "woman of letters." But
such a term, used without pejorative implication, is a reasonably exact
description of her status in society. Although Franklin conceives her as
having womanly traits, she is relatively desexed and unclassed, a partici-
pant in her society and yet the observer of it. She is significantly aware
furthermore, of her role as self-made author whose authority to write—
the right to be an author—derives from her self-admission into the Third
Realm. The most substantial essay Silence writes in her brief career is, as
a matter of fact, a satirical commentary on the changing nature of this
authority. This takes the form of a well-known satire on Harvard College
in the fourth number of the *Dogood Papers.*

Silence, who has been urged by Clericus, a clergyman boarder in
her home, to give her son an education at Harvard, soon afterward seeks
her "usual Place of Retirement under the *Great Apple-Tree,*" where she
falls asleep and has a dream about the Temple of Learning. The "stately
edifice" turns out to be in fact a seat of dullness, inhabited by a tribe of

students who, finding that learning is difficult and demanding, make the ascent to the throne of Learning only through following well-established modes of cheating. The chief import of the dream vision is "the extream Folly of those Parents, who, blind to their Childrens Dulness, and insensible to the Solidity of their Skulls, because they think their Purses can afford it, will needs send them to the Temple of Learning, where for want of a suitable Genius, they learn little more than how to carry themselves handsomely, and enter a Room genteely, (which might as well be aquir'd at a Dancing-School,) and from whence they return, after Abundance of Trouble and Charge, as great Blockheads as ever, only more proud and self-conceited." Silence, it is to be noted, does not discover in her vision that college is a worthless institution, merely that its true value is limited to the few who have the capacity for it. But the poor among these few cannot gain admittance. The entrance to the Temple of Learning must be made past two guards: Riches, who admits applicants who can pay; and Poverty, who denies those who cannot. The result is the bourgeois employment of the college as a finishing school. And yet hidden in the satire on the corruption of the true meaning of learning by money values is a revelation of a profound change in the relation of letters and learning to society. This occurs when Silence makes the curious discovery that Learning "in awful State" on her "magnificent Throne" is "very busily employ'd in writing something on a half a Sheet of Paper." Upon inquiry Silence is told that Learning is "preparing a Paper, call'd *The New-England Courant.*" Meanwhile:

> On her Right Hand sat *English*, with a pleasant smiling Countenance, and handsomely attir'd; and on her left were seated several *Antique Figures* with their Faces vail'd. I was considerably puzzl'd to guess who they were, until one informed me, (who stood beside me,) that those Figures on her left Hand were *Latin, Greek, Hebrew,* &c. and that they were very much reserv'd, and seldom or never unvail'd their Faces here, and then to few or none, tho' most of those who have in this Place acquir'd so much Learning as to distinguish them from *English* pretended to an intimate Acquaintance with them. I then enquir'd of him, what could be Reason why they continu'd vail'd, in this Place especially: He pointed to the Foot of the Throne, where I saw *Idleness*, attended with *Ignorance*, and these (he informed me) were they, who first vail'd them, and still kept them so.[9]

This is a symbolization (it may well be the first in American literature) of the expansion of the Third Realm—of the triumph of the vernacular languages and of the periodical press. We note that the satire does not present Learning as prostituted to the press. On the contrary, Learning has accepted her new role as printer-editor-publisher of a newspaper. If Idleness and Ignorance have veiled the learned languages, they have not veiled the goddess herself. She still reigns. The implication is that the center of the Republic of Letters has shifted from the university to the printing shop and the self-made author like Silence Dogood. Franklin does not imagine his little satire as a miniature *Dunciad* about the progress of dullness, a triumphant inversion of a progress of literature.[10] He offers a kind of celebration of the freeing of letters and learning from the authority of the university, realizing at the same time that this has occurred at the expense of a certain degradation of this initial embodiment of the polity of letters.

The implied elevation of the role of the self-made author in Silence Dogood is still more forcibly, if more subtly, suggested in the character and work of the philomath Richard Saunders, the editor of *Poor Richard's Almanack*, which Franklin commenced in Philadelphia ten years after the brief run of the *Dogood Papers*. A poverty-stricken countryman who is a lover of learning, Poor Richard enters into the business of writing after, as he says, his wife has threatened "to burn all my Books and Rattling-Traps (as she calls my Instruments) if I do not make some profitable Use of them for the Good of my Family." With the assurance of a printer that he will derive "some considerable share of the Profits," Poor Richard begins the publication of an almanac.[11] The result is a decided easing of his economic condition. His improved circumstances are more confirmed than denied when after a few years of publication Poor Richard is found complaining that the printer is running away with most of the profits of the almanac enterprise. The real meaning of Poor Richard's grievance lies in his qualification of it: the printer, he adds, "is a Man I have a great Regard for, and I wish his Profit ten times greater than it is."[12] This suggestion of the identity of Poor Richard and Franklin is more than waggish humor. In Poor Richard, Franklin the printer and Franklin the man of letters are united—more than they are in Silence Dogood—as a representation of the expanding literacy of print. Poor Richard—purveyor of information, wit, and philosophical and scientific argument—embodies the domestication of the Third Realm in a world moving toward a democratic literacy inherent in the technology of print. (The full democratization of literacy would take place in the nineteenth century with the industrialization of the printing business.) Poor Richard, to be sure, recognizes the totality of the dominion of print and its replacement of the world of the manuscript and the oral mode; in four lines of doggerel verse which he offers as one of his quotations he says a farewell to the world of anonymous minstrels and bards and summarizes a world dominated by publication:

If you wou'd not be forgotten
As soon as you are dead and rotten,
Either write things worth reading
Or do things worth the writing.[13]

 The opening up of the Third Realm is symbolized more dramatically in *Poor Richard's Almanack* of 1746 in the identification of Poor Richard with the tradition of the literary rural retreat.

Who is *Poor Richard?* People oft inquire,
Where lives? What is he? never yet the nigher.
Somewhat to ease your Curiositee,
Take these slight Sketches of my Dame and me.
 Thanks to kind Readers and a careful Wife,
With plenty bless'd, I lead an easy Life;
My Business Writing; hers to drain the Mead,
Or crown the barren Hill with useful Shade;
In the smooth Glebe to see the Plowshare worn,
And fill the Granary with needful Corn.
Press nectareous Cyder from my loaded Trees,
Print the sweet Butter, turn the Drying Cheese.
Some Books we read, tho' few there are that hit
The happy Point where Wisdom joins with Wit;
That set fair Virtue naked to our View,
And teach us what is *decent,* what is *true.*
The Friend sincere, and honest Man, with Joy
Treating or treated oft our Time employ.
Our Table next, Meals temperate; and our Door
Op'ning spontaneous to the bashful Poor.
Free from the bitter Rage of Party Zeal,
All those we love who seek the publick Weal.[14]

 The image of Poor Richard on his farm pleasantly engaged in the "Business" of writing—while his wife tends to the agricultural tasks—presents a striking variation of the ideal of literary retirement. Poor Richard's mercenary literary activity may be regarded as a violation of the integrity of the idealized pastoral dominion of mind as this descends into eighteenth-century literature from Virgil and Horace. The location of the almanac maker's business in a pastoral setting may even be construed as a pastoral strategy—that is, as affording a pastoral ratification of Grubstreet, or bourgeois, enterprise. No doubt this motive exists in the depiction of Poor Richard's Pennsylvania Twickenham. But the complexity of Poor Richard must be taken into account. He is not only a hack but a man of letters and a moral preceptor. As a counselor in the use of money and time and the mutual relation thereof, he presents the idea that financial independence gained through intellectual work and the concept of pastoral leisure defined in literary tradition can be brought together. Poor Richard has earned his Arcadia, but it is not the less Arcadia. His affluence enhances his moral independence.

III

Two years before he forsook an active part in the business of printing and bookselling, Franklin established Poor Richard securely in a symbolic home of the moral philosopher and man of letters. This was, one surmises, a deliberate act on Franklin's part. Removed from the city and worldly affairs, Poor Richard becomes distinctly a voice carrying the authority of pastoral detachment. Although he identifies the literary vocation with that of the farmer and thus appears as a common man articulating the values of the common reader, Poor Richard is not fused with the common mind. For all his expression of bourgeois-democratic attitudes, he speaks from the Third Realm. In his representation of the literary vocation, knowledge, wisdom, and wit do not spring from common literacy. He does not equate the man *of* letters and the man *with* letters.

There is more than a little justification in holding that, with whatever wry, ironic humor, Poor Richard symbolizes in provincial microcosm the cosmopolitan figure of letters and learning Franklin was becoming during the years between the almanac maker's inception and the middle of the eighteenth century. This was the figure David Hume acclaimed in 1762 when he learned of the American's imminent departure from the post he had held in England as colonial agent of Pennsylvania. At this time Hume wrote to Franklin:

> I am very sorry, that you intend soon to leave our Hemisphere.
> America has sent us many good things, Gold, Silver, Sugar, Tobacco,
> Indigo, &c.: But you are the first Philosopher, and indeed the first
> Great Man of Letters for whom we are beholden to her: it is our
> own Fault that we have not kept him: Whence it appears that we do
> not agree with Solomon that Wisdom is above Gold: For we take
> care never to send back an ounce of the latter, which we once lay
> our Fingers upon.[15]

Hume's graceful but sincere compliment not only recognized Franklin as a peer of the Third Realm but also acknowledged the rise of the Republic of Letters in the colonial mind. But David Hume, it must be said, had little if any notion of the Franklin who wore the mask of

Poor Richard. Hume, who was fearful lest his theoretical destruction of the soul be bruited among the common people, considered speculation and knowledge to be the proper province of the community of the lettered—"a closed and interlocked system of mutual admiration and criticism," as Basil Willey described it. Hume knew the Franklin who invited colonial Americans "in circumstances that set them at Ease, and afford Leisure" to "cultivate the finer Arts, and improve the common Stock of Knowledge" by forming a society of "Virtuosi or ingenious men." This would be called the American Philosophical Society, and it would be dedicated to maintaining "a constant Correspondence" on a great variety of subjects.[16] Hume scarcely understood that in the eighteenth century the self-articulation of the Third Realm through the correspondence of the learned could not be separated from the widening literacy of print.

Still less did Hume understand that in this expansion of literacy the Great Critique of Church and State was being translated into an active politics of literacy. This was a politics based not on the idea of a conquest of illiteracy—of the achievement of a universal literacy by means of a gross diffusion of elementary reading and writing skills—but on the concept of achieving a universal freedom of the educated secular mind by means of an extension of the Republic of Letters and an enhancement of its historical reality. This would be accomplished through the larger association of men of letters in a worldwide community created by a diffusion of pamphlets, magazines, and books and through an increase of the influence of men of letters. Which is to say, through an increase in the persons they can influence—in the number of men *with* letters who can be directed in the formation of an informed public opinion. The goal of the politics of literacy as it took shape in the Age of the Enlightenment was the domination of Church and State by the Third Realm, or—if it cannot be put quite so explicitly—the domination of history based on a cosmopolitan acquirement of a rational power over nature and man. The quest for such a dominion—for a moral government of the world by men of letters—was rooted in the faith that nature and man exist in a rational and (because it is rational) a moral universe; either nature or man is subject to explication in a rational employment of language.

As it became increasingly localized in a multiplicity of institutions such as the French Academy, the Royal Society, and the American Philosophical Society, the Republic of Letters became a realm operating within the conjoined realms of Church and State—in a loose but vital way a symbolic *imperium in imperio* in Western civilization. But the Third Realm became world historical in a definite sense only when it became operative and active in the determination of events in specific historical situations, for example, that involving the relationship of the American colonies to the British Empire.

IV

Representing the American expression of the Third Realm as an *imperium in imperio* of the British Empire, Franklin assumed his full role as a world historical man of letters. Or, it is possibly more accurate to say, as a world historical printer. For in Franklin's view the vocation of the man of letters subsumed the vocation of the printer, that is, in the case of the printer as Franklin knew him: the printer in the eighteenth-century printing house, a combined technician, editor, publisher, and bookseller. From the beginning of his career Franklin conceived the representation of the Third Realm in the Age of Print to be the leather-apron man at the printing press screw. (As in the age of the manuscript the Third Realm had been represented by the figure of the copyist in the *scriptorum*.) Franklin's sense of the communication of the word was that it depends on the skill and integrity with which it is reproduced and disseminated. The politics of literacy—the examination of the truth of Church and State in a free debate of ideas—is singularly subject to how the printer regards his moral responsibility to his task. Franklin made a declaration of his moral commitment to printing in 1731, when, under pressure of an attack on his own press, he wrote "An Apology for Printers." Among the particulars of Franklin's defense of printers the following are exceptionally noteworthy:

> Printers are educated in the Belief, that when Men differ in
> Opinion, both sides ought equally to have the Advantage of being
> heard by the Publick; and that when Truth and Error have fair
> Play, the former is always an overmatch for the latter: Hence they
> chearfully serve all contending Writers that pay them well, without
> regarding on which side they are of the Question in Dispute.
> Being thus continually employ'd in serving both Parties, Printers
> naturally acquire a vast Unconcernedness as to right or wrong
> Opinions contain'd in what they print; regarding it only as the
> Matter of their daily labour: They print things full of Spleen and
> Animosity, with the utmost Calmness and Indifference, and without
> the least Ill-will to the Persons reflected on; who nevertheless
> unjustly think the Printer as much their Enemy as the Author, and
> join them both together in their Resentment.
> That it is unreasonable to imagine Printers approve of every thing
> they print, and to censure them on any particular thing accordingly;
> since in the way of their Business they print such great variety of
> things opposite and contradictory. It is likewise as unreasonable
> what some assert, *That Printers ought not to print any Thing but*

what they approve, since if all of that Business should make such a Resolution, and abide by it, an End would thereby be put to Free Writing, and the World would afterwards have nothing to read but what happen'd to be the Opinion of Printers.[17]

Yet another major particular in Franklin's list of ten in "An Apology for Printers" concerns the limits of a printer's moral tolerance.

That notwithstanding what might be urg'd in behalf of a Man's being allow'd to do in the Way of his Business whatever he is paid for, yet Printers do continually discourage the Printing of great Numbers of bad things, and stifle them in the Birth. I my self have constantly refused to print anything that might countenance Vice, or promote Immorality; tho' by complying in such Cases with the corrupt Taste of the Majority I might have got much Money. I have also always refus'd to print such things as might do real Injury to any Person, how much soever I have been solicited, and tempted with Offers of Great Pay; and how much soever I have by refusing got the Ill-will of those who would have employ'd me. I have hitherto fallen under the Resentment of large Bodies of Men, for refusing absolutely to print any of their Party or Personal Reflections. In this Manner I have made my self many Enemies, and the constant Fatigue of denying is almost insupportable. But the Publick being unacquainted with all this, whenever the poor Printer happens either through Ignorance or much Persuasion, to do any thing that is generally thought worthy of Blame, he meets with no more Friendship or Favour on the above Account, than if there were no Merit in't at all.[18]

A declaration of practice founded on his own experience, "An Apology for Printers" is as well a statement reflecting the experience of the Third Realm in its struggle for self-articulation in history. It is both a practical and a symbolic statement: an announcement of a clear differentiation of the Third Realm in colonial American history. From this point on, a colonial press—although it was always affected by governmental censorship—would provide for the localization of the politics of literacy in America. This is the development brilliantly described in Bernard Bailyn's *The Ideological Origins of the American Revolution.* Bailyn discovers a primary rationale of the American Revolution in a colonial pamphlet literature which afforded "the clarification and consolidation under the pressure of events of a view of the world and of America's place in it." This literature (Bailyn does not discuss it in quite the same terms used here) was an offshoot of the expansion of the Third

Realm in the England of the Commonwealth and of the Glorious Revolution. These were the ages of Milton, James Harrington, Henry Neville, and Algernon Sidney. The diffusion of the politics of literacy by these men of letters and "heroes of liberty" was carried further by their inheritors in the early eighteenth century. Among these were John Trenchard, Thomas Gordon, Bishop Hoadly, and other pamphleteers who followed a "country" as opposed to a London vision of government and social order and further widened the influence of the Third Realm. Reprinted by American printers, the English pamphleteers became the core of an American pamphlet literature that advanced the tendency to democratize the mind and prepared the way for the Revolution, not to speak of sustaining it once it began.[19]

Unifying the roles of printer and man of letters like no other figure in the eighteenth century, Franklin expressed the harmony and power—the hegemony—the Third Realm had achieved three centuries after the invention of printing. His assertion of the moral and intellectual power of the Republic of Letters is integral to its evolvement into world historical meaning in the Revolution and the founding of the new nation. And yet, like Voltaire, though unlike more exuberant intellectuals such as Condorcet, Franklin sensed the historical finitude of the Third Realm. His advocacy of the politics of literacy always conveys an indeterminate aura of ironic reservation about the quest for social order based on human wisdom, Franklin being constantly aware of the precarious balance between civilizational and barbaric impulses in man. His final statement about the liberty of the press is a pessimistic satire entitled "An Account of the Supremest Court of Judicature in Pennsylvania, Viz. The Court of the Press." In a time when the liberty of the press has become an unquestionable assumption of society, the sole recourse of the individual who is singled out for condemnation by its arbitrary decision may be, Franklin suggests, to take up a cudgel against printer and author. The violation of the civility of freedom by the press, in Franklin's satirical view at any rate, justifies a liberty of the bludgeon on the part of the victimized individual. But Franklin was disposed to think that man's capacity to create a literary and intellectual realm of existence expressed an ancient opposition to barbarism as inherent in his nature as the inclination to barbarism. He died believing that the God of the universe had conferred the possibility of "Government by human Wisdom"[20] on mankind, and that this possibility could be realized through the agency of the Third Realm. "God grant," he wrote almost at the end, "that not only the love of liberty, but a thorough knowledge of the rights of man, may pervade the nations of the earth, so that a philosopher may set his foot anywhere on its surface, and say, 'This is my country.'"[21]

NOTES

1. Quoted in Carl Van Doren, *Benjamin Franklin* (New York: Garden City Publishing Company, 1941), p. 123.

2. Ibid., p. 123. Epitaph quoted on p. 124.

3. Christopher Dawson, *Religion and the Rise of Western Culture* (New York: Image Books, 1958), pp. 197, 204. The theory of history advanced by Eric Voegelin is basic to an understanding of the Third Realm. See especially his *The New Science of Politics: An Introduction* (Chicago: University of Chicago Press, 1952), pp. 107–32. Bizarre though they may be at times, the theories of Marshall McLuhan must be recognized as highly significant. See in particular *The Gutenberg Galaxy: The Making of Typographic Man* (Toronto: University of Toronto Press, 1962). Also see Lewis P. Simpson, "Literary Ecumenicalism of the American Enlightenment," in *The Ibero-American Enlightenment*, ed. A. Owen Aldridge (Urbana: University of Illinois Press, 1971), pp. 317–32; Simpson, "Federalism and the Crisis of Literary Order," *American Literature*, 32 (November 1960), 253–66; and Simpson, "The Satiric Mode: The Early National Wits," in *The Comic Imagination in American Literature*, ed. Louis D. Rubin, Jr. (New Brunswick: Rutgers University Press, 1973), pp. 49–61.

4. Michael Walzer, *The Revolution of the Saints: A Study in the Origins of Radical Politics* (New York: Atheneum, 1968), p. 124.

5. Franklin, *Autobiography and Other Writings*, ed. Russel B. Nye (Boston: Houghton Mifflin, 1958), pp. 10–13. A detailed and interesting study of Franklin's journalistic career—from a point of view different from that stressed in the present essay—is to be found in James A. Sappenfield, *A Sweet Instruction: Franklin's Journalism as a Literary Apprenticeship* (Carbondale: Southern Illinois University Press, 1973).

6. Ibid., p. 15.

7. Ibid., p. 19.

8. *The Papers of Benjamin Franklin*, ed. Leonard W. Labaree, et al. (New Haven: Yale University Press, 1959–), I, 9. Referred to hereafter as *Papers*.

9. *Papers*, I, 15–16.

10. See Aubrey L. Williams, *Pope's Dunciad: A Study of Its Meaning* (Baton Rouge: Louisiana State University, 1955), esp. pp. 42–59.

11. *Papers*, I, 311.

12. *Papers*, II, 218.

13. *Papers*, II, 194.

14. *Papers*, III, 60. Important aspects of the retirement theme in the eighteenth century are discussed in Maynard Mack, *The Garden and the City: Retirement and Politics in the Later Poetry of Pope, 1731–1743* (Toronto: University of Toronto Press, 1969).

15. *Papers*, X, 81–82.

16. Basil Willey, *The Eighteenth Century Background: Studies in the Idea of Nature in the Thought of the Period* (Boston: Beacon Press, 1961), p. 123. Also, see page 122. *Papers*, II, 380–81.

17. *Papers*, I, 195.

18. *Papers*, I, 196.

19. Bernard Bailyn, *The Ideological Origins of the American Revolution* (Cambridge: Belknap Press of Harvard University Press, 1967), pp. 22–54,

160–229. Also, see Peter Gay, *The Enlightenment: An Interpretation* (New York: Alfred A. Knopf, 1969), II, 555–68.

20. "Motion for Prayers in Convention," in *Benjamin Franklin: Representative Selections,* ed. Frank Luther Mott and Chester E. Jorgenson (New York: American Book Company, 1936), p. 490. Franklin made this motion in the Constitutional Convention, June 28, 1787.

21. Quoted in Nye, "Introduction" to *Autobiography and Other Writings,* pp. xvii–xviii.

Bruce I. Granger

❦ Franklin as
Press Agent in England

It is well known that from 1757 to 1762 and again from 1764 to 1775 Benjamin Franklin was a colonial agent in England. Not generally known at the time was the fact that during this period he contributed over one hundred letters to the English press. In the journalistic practice of the eighteenth century the letter to the press, or editorial, enjoyed prestige as a literary form from as early as the 1720s when Thomas Gordon and John Trenchard defended radical Whiggery in a series of letters signed "Cato." Half a century later the antiministerial letters of "Junius" achieved international fame. Franklin's letters let us glimpse the man in a more informal posture than his official duties allowed him to assume, and reveal him as a political moderate who, in language more homespun than legalistic, put the welfare of America ahead of that of England whenever the interests of the two clashed.

Verner W. Crane points out that the English newspapers and magazines provided Franklin the journalist "with ample scope for political writing—and also with a remarkable freedom of expression."[1] No fewer than thirty of his letters first appeared in the *London Chronicle*, printed by his longtime friend William Strahan. Henry Sampson Woodfall, publisher of what was probably the finest English daily, the *Public Advertiser*, carried forty of Franklin's letters, conniving at all of his newspaper hoaxes in England. In a letter to the public, Woodfall voiced

21

the principle of the open forum which then prevailed in England: "The
Public Advertiser is open to all Parties, and my Correspondents have
ever been at Liberty to make it what they please. If I am discovered
sometimes to be too ministerial, at others my Readers will confess I am
sufficiently free with Ministers."[2]

Franklin the colonial agent was well circumstanced to operate—
unofficially, to be sure—as press agent also. And well qualified, too. He
described himself in one letter, and it was no overstatement, as "one who
had lived long in America, knew the people and their affairs extremely
well—and was equally well acquainted with the temper and practices of
government officers."[3] Ministerial writers he characterized as "your
coffee-house talkers . . . mere rhetoricians, tongue-pads and scribes . . .
ever bawling for war on the most trifling occasions, and . . . the most
blood-thirsty of mankind."[4] One of them, probably John Mein, called him
in turn "this living emblem of Iniquity in Grey Hairs."[5] When this war
of words waxed hottest in the press he took his own advice most to heart:
"Passion, Invective and Abuse, serve no Cause. They show that a Man is
angry; but not always that he has reason to be angry."[6] And indeed his
own sweet reasonableness never deserted him. What he said of two well-
known letters to the English press, "An Edict by the King of Prussia" and
"Rules by Which a Great Empire May be Reduced to a Small One,"
holds equally for all of them: "Such papers may seem to have a tendency to increase our divisions; but I intend a contrary effect, and hope
by comprising in little room, and setting in a strong light the grievances
of the colonies, more attention will be paid to them by our administra-
tion, and that when their unreasonableness is generally seen, some of
them will be removed to the restoration of harmony between us."[7]

In his progress from provincial to intercolonial to imperial statesman Franklin ever showed himself to be a federalist. By 1766 he had
come to that view of empire he would hold until the spring of 1775
when he declared for independence. The American colonies he envis-
ioned as member states in a British commonwealth of nations, autonomous except for the allegiance they owed the Crown. Although such a
view conflicted with the principle of Parliamentary sovereignty being
reasserted by the Grenville, Townshend, and North ministries, he held
to it firmly throughout the years of his second agency. "The British
empire," he declared in 1770, "is not a single state; it comprehends many;
and though the parliament of Great Britain has arrogated to itself the
power of taxing the colonies, it has no more right to do so, than it has to
tax Hanover. We have the same king, but not the same legislatures."[8]
Whatever his immediate objective, whether working for repeal of the
Stamp Act and Townshend Revenue Act or trying to prevent passage of
the Coercive Acts, this dominion view of empire underlay the particular

argument. His task was made more difficult by the fear of conspiracy which colored both sides of the Revolutionary controversy; as Edmund Burke wrote in 1769, "The Americans have made a discovery, or think they have made one, that we mean to oppress them: we have made a discovery, or think we have made one, that they intend to rise in rebellion against us. . . . we know not how to advance; they know not how to retreat. . . . Some party must give way."[9]

Franklin did not argue from legal precedent but appealed to that reason he thought fixed and universal in human nature. So it was that, when confronted with America's claims to legislative autonomy, he readily admitted, "I am not Lawyer enough to decide this question."[10] One such lawyer was John Dickinson, who in his *Letters from a Farmer in Pennsylvania* (1767–68) drew a distinction between revenue and regulation in an effort to prove the unconstitutionality of the Townshend Revenue Act. Whereupon Franklin wrote his son William:

> I know not . . . what bounds the Farmer sets to the power he
> acknowledges in Parliament to "regulate the trade of the colonies,"
> it being difficult to draw lines between duties for regulation and
> those for revenue. . . . The more I have thought and read on the
> subject the more I find myself confirmed in opinion, that no middle
> doctrine can be well maintained, I mean not clearly with intelligible
> arguments. Something might be made of either of the extremes;
> that Parliament has a power to make *all laws* for us, or that it has
> a power to make *no laws* for us; and I think the arguments for the
> latter more numerous and weighty than those for the former.[11]

When compared with the "Colonist's Advocate" letters wherein Franklin argued for repeal of the same Act, the *Farmer's Letters* are weighted with legal proofs. The one man argues his case pragmatically, the other from constitutional, charter, and natural rights.

Franklin made the letter to the press into a more flexible vehicle for argument serious and satirical than did his English contemporary, "Junius." When not drafted as conventional letters to the editor, they are conceived as anecdote, annotations, a list of queries, or cast in a more belletristic form like colloquy, fable, parody, fictitious controversy, or fictitious extract.[12] In contrast to the essentially lighthearted, social tone of his periodical essays and almanac writings, he approached his duties as press agent in dead earnest. In the half century separating the *Dogood Papers* from the letters to the press his manner took on a deeper and more elusive coloring. Not that he ever abandoned completely the urbanity early acquired from the example of Addison, in underlying organization these later writings resemble more nearly the manner of Defoe and Swift.

One rhetorical device employed by Defoe and Swift is political arithmetic. In 1768, when American resistance to the Townshend Acts was stiffening, Franklin used this device in an attack on warmongers: "Contractors, jobbing mercantile members of parliament, officers starving on half pay, and gunsmiths who *toast . . . a speedy and a perpetual war,* may wish, rather than no war at all, for a *civil* one in America." No matter how vigorously England may pursue such a war, I compute that "it will not be so soon terminated as some folks would have us believe." In the Seven Years' War "*one* of the *fifteen* Colonies we now have there (and one far short of being the strongest) held out *five years* against *twenty five thousand* British regular troops, joined by *twenty-five thousand* Colonists . . . and aided by a strong fleet of men of war."[13]

> Now supposing that the twenty five thousand Colonists, that then joined us, should hereafter be against us, and that this makes no difference, and considering that instead of *one* Colony to conquer, we are to have *fifteen,* . . . this, by my computation, will amount to just *seventy-five* years. I hope Messieurs the company of gunsmiths will for the present be so good as to be content with a civil war of *seventy-five* years, as perhaps we may scarce be able to afford them a *perpetual* one.[14]

Franklin here writes as a humble English tradesman, one of "us poor devils that live by manufactures or by trade," in order to lend verisimilitude to this arithmetical argument against war.

Another popular device is the historical equation. At a time when many Englishmen were championing Paoli and the cause of Corsica against an invading French army, Franklin issued the following fictitious extract "from Paris to a Gentleman in London":

> You English consider us French as Enemies to Liberty: You reproach us for endeavouring to reduce Corsica to our Obedience. . . . The Corsicans are not so remote from us as the Americans are from you; they never enriched us by their Labour and their Commerce; they never engaged in our Wars, and fought as Brothers, Side by Side with us, and for us, bleeding in the same Cause; they never loved and honoured us; they are not *our* Children.
>
> Yet at this very moment, while you are abusing us for attempting to reduce the Corsicans, you yourselves are about to make Slaves of a much greater Number of those British Americans. . . . All the Liberty you seem to value, is the Liberty of abusing your Superiors, and of tyrannizing over those below you.[15]

Posing as a Frenchman, Franklin constructs the equation: America is to

England as Corsica is to France: to point up a more serious example of freedom imperiled.

The most important of the rhetorical devices that color Franklin's letters to the press and help unify certain of them is the pseudonym. It is understandable that he should have drawn the veil of anonymity over his political writings during this period; in addition to being colonial agent for several provinces, he was joint deputy postmaster-general for the colonies. The pseudonym not only effectively concealed from the official class what his left hand was doing but sometimes renders the satire, when his intention is satiric, ironical. Moreover, such pseudonymity enabled him to mediate between extremes of political opinion and at the same time assess the differences more objectively; for, as he had observed years before, "When the Writer conceals himself, he has the Advantage of hearing the Censure both of Friends and Enemies, express'd with more Impartiality."[16]

Some of the letters are written in an assumed American, many more in an English character. One conciliatory letter opens with feigned modesty, "I am an American Gentleman, and as yet not entirely acquainted with the Customs of my dear Mother Country."[17] Another defending America against British ignorance and misrepresentation concludes, "I shall therefore boldly say, that the English are brave and wise; the Scotch are brave and wise; and the people of the British colonies, proceeding from both nations—I would say the same of them, if it might not be thought vanity."[18] Over the signature "New-England," his most fully developed American character, Franklin introduces himself to the printer as "a native of Boston, in New-England." Alluding to Boston-born Barlow Trecothick, who was then standing for Parliament, he continues: "I sit down, Sir, after much patience, merely to take some notice of the invective and abuse, that have, on this occasion, been so liberally bestowed on my country, by your writers who sign themselves *Old England, a Londoner, a Liveryman of London,* &c. &c. [By the way, Mr. Printer, should I have said liberally or illiberally? Not being now it seems allowed to be an Englishman, I ought modestly to doubt my English, and submit it as I do to your correction.]" Though I may recriminate a little against "the productions of a few unknown angry writers, heated by an election contest, who rave against America, because a candidate they would decry once lived there," I assure you, "Boston man as I am, Sir, and inimical, as my country is represented to be, I hate neither England nor Englishmen, driven (though my ancestors were) by mistaken oppression of former times, out of this happy country, to suffer all the hardships of an American wilderness."[19]

Crane maintains that Franklin "was shrewdly aware that his arguments for American rights would gain in effect if they seemed to come from a less interested source; on occasion he posed . . . as an Englishman with neither kinsfolk nor property across the sea."[20] Again in a conciliatory mood he concludes a letter on American longevity:

> I have myself lately travelled over the greater part of that extensive continent; and can with truth say . . . that I could not discover among that whole people, one grain of disaffection to their brethren in Britain, nor did I meet with a single person who had ever formed the most distant idea of throwing off their allegiance to the mother country. This it is doing them but bare justice to declare; and is all the return I can at present make them for the kindness and hospitality with which, purely on account of my being an *Old England-Man,* I was universally treated.[21]

It was as "The Colonist's Advocate," the only instance in which he carried a pseudonym through a series of letters, that Franklin developed an English character most fully, though in contrast to Dickinson's Pennsylvania Farmer this character remains shadowy. Keenly aware that within the English official class there was widespread ignorance of the American colonies and indifference to colonial interests, this advocate for total repeal of the Townshend Revenue Act sought to win the confidence of his English readers at once by assuring them, "The impartial Publick will judge, from my Manner of treating the Subject, in the following Numbers, . . . what Opportunities I have had, during some Years Service in America, of knowing the Inclinations, Affections ,and Concerns of the Inhabitants in the Provinces of that extensive Continent."[22] Trusting that the British nation will hear him out, the Advocate frankly pleads the cause of America in his fourth letter: "To assume the Title of the *Colonist's Advocate,* is to undertake the Defence of Three Millions of the most valuable Subjects of the British Empire, against Tyranny and Oppression, brought upon them by a wrong-headed Ministry. . . . I beg Justice for those brave People, who, in Confidence of our Protection, left their native Country, pierced into Woods, where no humanized Foot had, from the Creation, trod; . . . [and] have made us the Envy and Terror of Europe."[23] After the eleventh letter the Advocate broke off his suit, for at this juncture Lord North's motion in Commons to retain the three-pence tax on tea convinced Franklin that total repeal would be defeated. As indeed it was.

As English journalists from the turn of the century had so conclusively shown, the persona or mask can be made to serve the cause of satire well. Among Augustan writers none excelled Swift in the use of this device. Without arguing for direct influence, it can be demonstrated that Franklin's ironic masks, like those of Swift, frequently assume the character of a spectator. When Franklin adopts this role he sometimes appears as impartial historian, sometimes as modest proposer. In *The Battle of the Books* Swift establishes the mask of impartial historian by having the author say of himself, "I, being possessed of all Qualifications requisite in an *Historian,* and retained by neither Party; have resolved to comply with the urgent *Importunity of my Friends,* by writing down a full impartial Account thereof."[24] In *Causes of the American Discontents before 1768* Franklin imposes on himself the task of being "an impartial historian of American facts and opinions."[25] Frequently he invests this mask with naiveté, as when he writes in defense of his Canada pamphlet: "[It] seem'd so full and clear, that I made up my Mind upon it. . . . But here comes an apparently sensible Writer from Bath . . . that perplexes me with an Assurance that the Doctrines of that Piece are *'big with Mischief,'* . . . that its Reasonings are *fallacious.*"[26] His well-meaning correspondent writes from Danzig, "We have long wondered here at the supineness of the English nation, under the Prussian impositions upon its trade entering our port," and encloses Frederick the Great's edict "Given at Potsdam, this twenty-fifth day of the month of August, one thousand seven hundred and seventy-three, and in the thirty-third year of our reign," which makes the same imperial demands of England that England had for years been making of her American colonies. In a postscript the correspondent manages to convey the impression of being simply an impartial witness to the matter at hand:

> Some take this Edict to be merely one of the King's *Jeux d'Esprit*: others suppose it serious, and that he means a quarrel with England; but all here think the assertion it concludes with, "that these regulations are copied from acts of the English parliament respecting their colonies," a very injurious one; it being impossible to believe, that a people distinguished for their love of liberty, a nation so wise, so liberal in its sentiments, so just and equitable towards its neighbours, should, from mean and injudicious views of petty immediate profit, treat its own children in a manner so arbitrary and tyrannical![27]

So plausible was the tone of this edict that, like Defoe's *Shortest Way with the Dissenters,* it deceived many readers when it first appeared.[28] It was perhaps Franklin's very success in the role of impartial historian that led him to complain, "Being born and bred in one of the countries, and having lived long, and made many agreeable connections of friendship in the other , I wish all prosperity to both; but . . . I do not find that I have gained any point in either country, except that of rendering myself suspected by my impartiality; in England of being too much an American, and in America of being too much an Englishman."[29]

Franklin felt equally at home in the Swiftian guise of modest proposer. Sometimes he used it incidentally, as when in his Canada pamphlet he writes: "If it be, after all, thought necessary to *check* the growth of our colonies . . . let an act of parliament, [then] be made, enjoining the colony midwives to stifle in the birth every third or fourth child. By this means you may keep the colonies to their present size."[30] Franklin's favorite among his letters to the English press was "Rules by Which a Great Empire May be Reduced to a Small One," wherein "A modern simpleton," addressing himself "to all ministers who have the management of extensive dominions," but especially to the "late minister" Lord Hillsborough, sets down as rules what were in fact colonial griev-ances of recent memory, and promises that if the ministers practice "these few *excellent rules* of mine," they will "get rid of the trouble of govern-ing" all their provinces.[31] In the spring of 1774, when Parliament was drafting coercive measures against Massachusetts, Franklin proposed that this letter be reprinted: "As I apprehend this plan is at present under the consideration of the House of Commons, I think a re-publication of it, at this time, would not be improper. The rules appear to me to be admirably adapted to the end proposed."[32]

In view of the ad hoc nature of Franklin's letters to the press two have been chosen for closer examination because they center on a topic that can be understood with a minimum of historical background: British military arrogance. Early in 1766, a few days before the debate in Com-mons on repeal of the Stamp Act, Franklin over the signature "Pacificus" offered a proposal for resolving the controversy "between the Mother Country and their rebellious American Children": "There are some Persons besides the Americans so amazingly stupid, as to distinguish in this Dispute between *Power* and *Right*, as tho' the former did not always imply the latter. . . . The American Plea of *Right*, their Appeal to Magna Charta, must of course be set aside; and I make no Doubt but the Grand Council of the Nation will at all Hazards insist upon an absolute Sub-mission to the Tax imposed upon them." In view of the fact that the Americans, "Descendants of your Pymms, Hampdens, and others of the like Stamp, . . . will not tamely give up what they call their natural, their constitutional Rights," I have a plan for coercing America which cannot fail, one so cheap that even Mr. George Grenville, "that great Oecono-mist," can "have no reasonable Objection to it." It is to transport "Two Thousand Highlanders . . . [if] Roman Catholics, the better . . . early in the Spring to Quebec: They with the Canadians, natural Enemies to our Colonists, . . . might make a Body of Five or Six Thousand Men; and I doubt not, by artful Management, and the Value of two or three Thou-sand Pounds in Presents, with the Hopes of Plunder, as likewise a Gratu-ity for every Scalp, the Savages on the Frontiers might be engaged to join, at least they would make a Diversion, which could not fail of being useful." From Canada this expedition might fall upon the Americans when they least expected it, burn their capitals, cut the throats of men, women, and children and scalp them, and destroy all their shipping. I think it best that British regulars remain neutral, "as it is to be feared they would be rather backward in embruing their Hands in the Blood of their Brethren and Fellow Subjects." "No Man in his Wits, after such terrible Military Execution, will refuse to purchase stamp'd Paper. If any one should hesitate, five or six Hundred Lashes in a cold frosty Morning would soon bring him to Reason." Pacificus concludes: "If the Massacre should be objected to, as it would too much depopulate the Country, it may be replied, . . . that, together with the Felons from our Gaols, we should soon be enabled to transport such Numbers to repeople the Colonies, as to make up for any Deficiency which Example made it Necessary to sacrifice for the Public Good. Great Britain might then reign over a loyal and submissive People, and be morally certain, that no Act of Parliament would ever after be disputed."[33] Masking as a peace-loving Englishman, Franklin here innocently declares, "I shall think myself happy if I can furnish any Hints that may be of public Utility," and proceeds with apparent good humor and impartiality to propose a plan for the conquest of America so devastatingly thorough as (so he hoped) to prick the conscience of the most hardened minister of state. Having failed to anticipate the tempest that arose in America over the Stamp Act, he is making amends by exercising his very considerable talent for irony, arguing for repeal of the Stamp Act more bluntly than he would in an examination before the House of Commons a fortnight hence.

In the spring of 1774, as Franklin recollected years later, a certain General Clarke boasted in his hearing that "with a Thousand British grenadiers, he would undertake to go from one end of America to the other, and geld all the Males, partly by force and partly by a little Coaxing."[34] Whereupon Franklin over the signature "A Freeholder of Old Sarum" suggested a "most feasible Method of humbling our rebellious Vassals of North America": In view of the fact that the Americans may eventually deny our authority altogether, "more especially when it is considered that they are a robust, hardy People, encourage early Marriages, and their Women being amazingly prolific, they must of consequence in 100 years be very numerous, and of course be able to set us at Defiance," it is humbly proposed that "a Bill be brought in and passed, and Orders immediately transmitted to G[enera]l G[ag]e, our Commander in Chief in North America, in consequence of it, that all Males there be c—st—ed."

Let a Company of Sow-gelders, consisting of 100 Men, accompany the Army, On their Arrival at any Town or Village, let Orders be

given that on the blowing of the Horn all the Males be assembled
in the Market Place. If the Corps are Men of Skill and Ability in
their Profession, they will make great Dispatch, and retard but
very little the Progress of the Army. . . . the most notorious
Offenders, such as Hancock, [Sam] Adams, &c. who have been the
Ringleaders in the Rebellion of our Servants, should be shaved
quite close. . . . It is true, Blood will be shed, but probably not
many Lives lost. Bleeding to a certain Degree is salutary. The
English, whose Humanity is celebrated by all the World, but
particularly by themselves, do not desire the Death of the
Delinquent, but his Reformation.

Consider the advantages arising from the execution of this scheme:

In the Course of fifty years it is probable we shall not have one
rebellious Subject in North America. This will be laying the Axe
to the root of the Tree. In the meantime a considerable Expence
may be saved to the Managers of the Opera, and our Nobility and
Gentry be entertained at a cheaper Rate by the fine Voices of our
own C—st—i, and the Specie remain in the Kingdom, which now,
to an enormous Amount, is carried every Year into Italy. It might
likewise be of service to our Levant Trade, as we could supply the
Grand Signor's Seraglio, and the Harams of the Grandees of the
Turkish Dominions with Cargos of Eunuchs, as also with Handsome
Women, for which America is as famous as Circassia.[35]

Franklin exploits the implications of Clarke's boast with a coarseness
that was native to him, taking care at every ironic turn to stay within the
realm of the possible. There is further irony in the fact that the speaker
is from Old Sarum, one of the rotten boroughs still represented in Parliament. Here as so often in the past Franklin's sense of timing is faultless:
a letter to the press at the time the Coercive Acts were being signed into
law might give English readers pause.

In his letters to the English press, many of which were reprinted
in America,[36] Franklin reached beyond the leather-apron class at Boston
and Philadelphia, for whom his essays and almanacs had first of all been
intended, to a far larger, transatlantic audience. In order to sway this
Anglo-American public in the prewar decade to the view that the American colonies should be granted dominion status within the British Empire,
he favored polemic statement to urbane, arguing his case seriously or
satirically as the occasion seemed to demand. Looking back on his
English agency, he wrote a friend in 1777, "I long laboured in England,
with great zeal and sincerity, to prevent the breach that has happened,
and which is now so wide, that no endeavours of mine can possibly heal

it."[37] The fact that his efforts as press agent at London ended in failure in no sense diminishes the literary merit of these political writings. For clarity, vigor, and humor of expression they represent journalism of a high order. Even so uncongenial a colleague as John Adams, his fellow commissioner in France, could not withhold tribute: "He had a satire that was good-natured or caustic, Horace or Juvenal, Swift or Rabelais, at his pleasure. He had talents for irony, allegory, and fable, that he could adapt with great skill to the promotion of moral and political truth."[38]

NOTES

1. Verner W. Crane, ed., *Benjamin Franklin's Letters to the Press, 1758–1775* (Chapel Hill: University of North Carolina Press, 1950), p. xix. Referred to hereafter as Crane.

2. *Public Advertiser*, Jan. 1, 1771, quoted in Fred J. Hinkhouse, *The Preliminaries of the American Revolution as Seen in the English Press 1763–1775* (New York: Columbia University Press, 1926), p. 13.

3. *The Papers of Benjamin Franklin*, ed. Leonard W. Labaree, et al. (New Haven: Yale University Press, 1959–), XIV, 102. Referred to hereafter as *Papers*.

4. *Papers*, XIV, 103.

5. Crane, p. 248.

6. *Papers*, XV, 110.

7. Albert Henry Smyth, ed., *The Writings of Benjamin Franklin*, VI (New York and London: Macmillan, 1906), 153. Referred to hereafter as Smyth.

8. *Papers*, XVII, 233.

9. Quoted in Bernard Bailyn, *The Ideological Origins of the American Revolution* (Cambridge: Belknap Press of Harvard University Press, 1967), pp. 158–59.

10. *Papers*, XV, 235.

11. *Papers*, XV, 75–76.

12. Anecdotes: *Papers*, XIII, 38–39, 183–84; Crane, p. 238. Annotations: *Papers*, VIII, 340–56; XII, 413–16, XIII, 45–49, 63–66; XV, 18–19. Queries: *Papers*, VIII, 163–68; XV, 187–89, 206–10; XVII, 266–68. Colloquy: *Papers*, XVII, 37–44; Smyth, VII, 82–86. Fable: *Papers*, XVII, 3–4. Parody: Smyth, VI, 118–24, 299–301; Crane, pp. 279–82. Fictitious controversy: *Papers*, XII, 123–24; 132–35; XV, 193–95. Fictitious extract: *Papers*, IX, 342–47; XVI, 19–20.

13. The one colony is Quebec; the other that is added to the familiar thirteen is presumably Nova Scotia.

14. *Public Advertiser*, Aug. 25, 1768; reprinted in *Papers*, XV, 191–93. For other examples of political arithmetic see *Papers*, VIII, 214–15; Smyth, V, 456–57.

15. *Public Advertiser*, Jan. 17, 1769; reprinted in *Papers*, XVI, 19–20. In two other letters Franklin constructs the following equations: English coffeehouse orators are to America as Athenian orators are to Sicily (*Papers*, XIV, 102–7); England is to Prussia as America is to England (Smyth, VI, 118–24).

16. *Papers*, I, 328.

17. *Papers,* XIII, 382.

18. *Papers,* VIII, 356.

19. *Papers,* XV, 63–67.

20. Verner W. Crane, "Certain Writings of Benjamin Franklin on the British Empire and the American Colonies," *Papers of the Bibliographical Society of America,* 27 (1934), 15.

21. *Papers,* XIV, 339.

22. *Papers,* XVII, 5–6.

23. *Papers,* XVII, 28.

24. Herbert Davis, ed., *The Prose Writings of Jonathan Swift,* I (Oxford: Blackwell, 1939), 145.

25. *Papers,* XV, 9.

26. *Papers,* IX, 110.

27. *Public Advertiser,* Sept. 22, 1773; reprinted in Smyth, VI, 118–24. For other instances of the impartial historian mask see *Papers,* VIII, 163–68; IX, 109–10; XV, 3–13; 110–12, 233–37.

28. See Franklin's letter of Oct. 6, 1773, to his son, Smyth, VI, 146.

29. *Papers,* XV, 272–73.

30. *Papers,* IX, 94–95.

31. *Public Advertiser,* Sept. 11, 1773; reprinted in Smyth, VI, 127–37. For other instances of the modest proposer mask see *Papers,* IX, 94–95; XIII, 55–58; Crane, pp. 232–33, 259–62, 262–64.

32. Crane, p. 258.

33. *Public Advertiser,* Jan. 26, 1766; reprinted in *Papers,* XIII, 55–58.

34. Smyth, IX, 261. Verner Crane says, "General Clarke was probably Col. Thomas Clarke, aide-de-camp to the King, commissioned Major-General in 1777 and Lieutenant-General in 1782" (*Letters to the Press,* p. 263n).

35. *Public Advertiser,* May 21, 1774; reprinted in Crane, pp. 262–64.

36. See for example John J. Zimmerman, "Benjamin Franklin and The Pennsylvania Chronicle," *Pennsylvania Magazine of History & Biography,* 81 (1957), 351–64, who discusses certain of Franklin's writings on the Stamp Act which William Goddard reprinted in the *Pennsylvania Chronicle* in 1767.

37. Smyth, VII, 47.

38. Charles Francis Adams, ed., *The Works of John Adams,* I (Boston: Little, Brown, 1850), 663.

Percy G. Adams

❧ Benjamin Franklin and the Travel-Writing Tradition

There were probably few people except sailors who in the eighteenth century traveled so much as Benjamin Franklin. In America, after leaving for Philadelphia at age seventeen, he returned to Boston a number of times. He went from place to place on the frontier helping to supply wagons for the fateful Braddock expedition and later supervising the building of forts during Bouquet's much more successful campaign. He traveled through every British colony in the New World, as he once said proudly, "almost from one end of the continent to the other." He went to Harvard, Yale, and William and Mary to accept M.A.'s and then doctorates. He left Philadelphia to confer with Indians at Easton, Albany, and Carlisle and years later to talk with General Washington, with his friendly enemy General Howe, and with the American army in Canada. In 1753, 1754–55, and 1763, his biggest travel years in America, he covered most of New England, New York, even Virginia and South Carolina.

But Franklin was a European too. He not only crossed the Atlantic Ocean eight times; he lived abroad in London and Paris for twenty-six years, Russel Nye estimates.[1] He went up and down England and across and back, he was in Wales twice, toured Scotland twice and Ireland once. He went to Tunbridge Wells, to the sea coast, often to Twyford or Cambridge or Oxford. From England he could jump to the continent. In 1761 he was in the Low Countries and in 1766 in Germany and Holland, while in 1767 and 1769 he went with his good friend Sir John

33

Pringle to Paris and Versailles. He did not, however, make two trips
attributed to him, one which Rudolph Eric Raspe seemed to think he
made to Switzerland in 1769 and one which Crèvecoeur said he took to
Franklin and Marshall College for commencement in 1787.[2] By my conservative estimate then, in a day without jets or interstates, before
steamships or trains, Franklin traveled well over 42,000 miles even if one
does not count the countless short trips he had to take from Philadelphia
to his farm in Burlington or from Passy to Versailles and Montmorency.
Furthermore, by another conservative estimate he spent over five years
of his life—a long one to be sure—as voyager, tourist, traveler, if we count
inns and necessary layovers and waits for ships, as we today count motel
nights or airport terminals and limousines.

This really amazing travel record, which may beat that of Franklin's energetic friend the evangelist George Whitefield, was compiled for
a number of reasons. As a family man he returned to visit his old home
and his relatives. As statesman he was a postmaster on long tours of
inspection; he was one of Pennsylvania's emissaries to the Iroquois or
helped organize defenses during Indian wars; he was the representative
of Congress to confer with generals; he was sent by Pennsylvania and
then other colonies to England; and he was Minister Plenipotentiary for
some nine years in Paris. As a scientist and man of letters he visited universities in America, in England, and on the Continent, or he visited other
scientists, such as Cadwallader Colden, or other writers, such as David
Hume. As a friend he accepted many invitations to travel some distance,
as when he often went to the Bishop of St. Asaph's at Twyford. But all
of these reasons for forcing him to make long trips were usually combined
with Franklin's tourist nature. He loved to travel for pleasure and profit,
he looked forward to it, it became almost a fetish to him. From 1723,
when he left Boston, until he was compelled to settle down at Passy in
1777, there are only five years in which he did not take an extended trip.
After long winter months in Philadelphia or London, he felt as he grew
older that his health and spirits demanded some kind of excursion. Over
and over he wrote his wife Deborah or his son William or certain friends
that "I begin to feel the want of my usual yearly Journeys" (to Deborah,
Aug. 7, 1761; *Papers*, IX, 337), or "I am as well as I can be without my
usual Journey, but I begin to feel the want of it, and shall out in a few
days, for a Tour of a few Weeks" (to Deborah, July 5, 1769; *Papers*,
XVI, 171), or "[I have] been us'd, as you know, to make a Journey once
a Year, the Want of which last Year has, I believe, hurt me" (to Deborah,
June 13, 1766; *Papers*, XIII, 316). And the complaint here is a typical one
for those few years he was unable to find a way to leave his job for weeks
at a time. In fact, near the end of his life the complaint is almost bitter
as he reported officially after his long service in France that during those

years "Mr. Franklin could make no journey for exercise, as has been annually his custom, and the confinement has brought on a malady that is likely to afflict him while he lives."[3]

Not only did he look forward to his trips or mutter when he failed to get them; he was vain about his tourist talents. During one of his two longest tours of the Eastern colonies he could brag to William Strahan in London that he had already traveled·1140 miles and "shall make" 640 more before reaching Philadelphia (Aug. 8, 1763; *Papers*, X, 320). After his Channel crossing on the way to Paris in 1767, he could gloat to Polly Stevenson about how the other, the inexperienced, travelers were all seasick and he was not (Sept. 14; *Papers*, XIV, 251). Following his second trip to Scotland, he wrote proudly of having taken "as long a Journey as a Man can well make in these Islands" (to Samuel Franklin, Jan. 13, 1772; Smyth, V, 370). Even at age seventy-six he seemed seriously to believe he could stand going by stagecoach through Italy, where he had never been (Smyth, IX, 42). And, finally, after arriving at Southampton before his last ocean voyage, he could brag once more that at age seventy-seven he had stood the trip from Paris better than had his two grandsons and M. le Viellard (Smyth, IX, 366). Franklin, then, not only enjoyed traveling and believed it beneficial to health and morale; he gloried in his own broad experience as a traveler.

Moreover, Franklin knew many famous travelers personally, was widely read in travel literature, eagerly looked forward to the plans for and results of well-known voyages, and no doubt his literary style was influenced by the style of travel writers. In America he was close to John Bartram, the botanist-traveler, to the ocean-hopping George Whitefield, to the French-American Crèvecoeur, to the Swedish naturalist Pierre Kalm. In England he performed experiments with Banks and Solander, who went on Cook's first voyage, knew intimately John R. Forster, who with his son went on Cook's second voyage, and met Cook himself, whose picture and journals he later received with great appreciation and for whom he wrote out a famous "passport" ordering American seaman during the Revolution to provide the great English navigator a safe passage. But Franklin knew English land travelers too, James Boswell, for example. And he owned and read many accounts of voyages, his interest being in scientific elements—natural history, for example—but also in customs and in national characteristics. We know that more than once he ordered maps and travel books (*Papers*, V, 392–93, e.g.), that he read of voyages to the north in search of a water route through Canada, that in 1772 he wrote his friend le Roy praising the French for sending two ships to the North Pole, and that in the next year he became interested in the Royal Society's two ships on a similar mission. He read Charlevoix (1744), Lockman's 1762 edition of the Jesuit travelers, and Bouguer's book on his and la Condamine's voyage to Peru (*Papers*, V, 468–69). He read "Ogilby," but how many of Ogilby's popular geographies derived from travel books we cannot be sure. Probably inspired by his very close friend and favorite correspondent John Bartram, he read William Stork's 1766 *An Account of East Florida* (Smyth, V, 336) and even Bossu's romantic *Travels through Louisiana* (Smyth, V, 336, 387). And he quoted William Dampier on Mindanao, paraphrased Pierre Kalm on early Norse settlements in America, and over and over in later life recommended Kalm's book and Crèvecoeur's *Letters from an American Farmer* (Smyth, VI, 68; 86–87; IX, 149–50).

His interest in people who traveled and in their books led him to back real voyages, to plan other voyage ventures, and to engage in important travel controversies. The real voyages he backed were those of the *Argo*, a ship captained by the former clerk of the *California*, one of two ships sent out by Arthur Dobbs in 1746 to search for a Northwest Passage. This clerk, now known to be Theodorous Swaine Drage, author of two travel books and a long-time acquaintance of Franklin, came to America and persuaded Governor Samuel Ogle of Maryland and, especially, Franklin to back him in 1753 and again in 1754 in two ventures in search of that same elusive Northwest Passage and the £20,000 Parliament was offering for its discovery. Drage's ability to persuade Franklin to invest huge sums of money was aided by the fact that Franklin was already convinced that such a waterway existed, as two letters to William Strahan in 1744 and 1745 attest. In the first, he rather ardently defended Arthur Dobbs in his notorious argument with Captain Christopher Middleton, who had sailed to Canada and was sure there was no Northwest Passage (*Papers*, II, 409–12). In fact, without even having read Middleton's arguments the normally fair-minded Franklin said he did not "much like" the man. In the second letter he thanked Strahan for sending a copy of Middleton's book but gave no hint that it had any effect on him.[4]

That Middleton's arguments and even Drage's two abortive voyages failed to convince Franklin and that Franklin was for much of his life almost obsessed with the notion, with the hope, of there being a Northwest Passage are evidenced by his becoming involved in another, even more famous, travel controversy, that concerning the spurious letter written by the equally spurious Admiral Bartholomew de Fonte, who claimed to have made a voyage through Canada from the Pacific to the Atlantic in 1640. The letter, first published in *The Monthly Miscellany* in London during 1708, and often reprinted, has been conclusively shown to be a hoax. But in the eighteenth century it was employed as a prime source, first by Dobbs and his man Drage, then by geographers such as the Englishman Emanuel Bowen in 1747 and the Frenchmen J. N. Delisle and Philippe Buache in 1750, then by writers in *The Gentleman's Magazine* over a period of years, and at last by Franklin in 1762, when to Pringle, his close friend and fellow member of the Royal Society, he wrote a long letter defending de Fonte. This letter, first published in 1957 and now included in the Yale edition of Franklin's *Papers* (X), is one of the most intriguing documents to come from the hand of Benjamin Franklin, for it shows him, one of the great hoaxers of all time, cogently arguing for the authenticity of a travel hoax, it shows him displaying prejudices and wishful thinking, even making mistakes he should not have made, but it also shows his great interest in and knowledge of voyages and voyage literature.[5]

There were more voyages planned and more travel controversies, however. In 1771 Franklin and Alexander Dalrymple, Hydrographer to the Admiralty, together drew up a "Plan for Benefiting Distant Unprovided Countries" by sending out a kind of "mercy" ship. Three years before, because he was not given the chief command of the expedition, Dalrymple had angrily refused to go on Cook's first voyage. Now he and Franklin planned for Dalrymple to command a vessel that would sail halfway around the world and take not only supplies but civilized engineering methods to ignorant savages. The expenses of the ship, to be supported by subscription, were carefully itemized and the nonprofit aim was announced:

> Many voyages have been undertaken with views of profit or of plunder, or to gratify resentment; to procure some advantage to ourselves, or to do some mischief to others. But a voyage is now proposed, to visit a distant people on the other side of the globe; not to cheat them, not to rob them, not to seize their lands, or enslave their persons; but merely to do them good, and make them, as far as in our power lies, to live as comfortably as ourselves.
> [Smyth, V, 340–44]

Although the "Plan," reprinted in Paris, elicited at least one subscription, the ship never sailed, Dalrymple was to be frustrated a second time in his hopes for a command to the South Seas, and Franklin, the projector, businessman, humanitarian, was never to sponsor a successful voyage, whether to northern or to southern waters.

Among the travel controversies Franklin engaged in after his mistake regarding de Fonte was one in which he spoke up for his friend John Hawkesworth's 1773 edition of the voyages of Byron, Wallis, Carteret, and Cook.[6] "It has been a Fashion," he complained to Jan Ingenhousz, "to decry Hawkesworth's Book; but it does not deserve the Treatment it has met with. It acquaints us with new People having new Customs, and teaches us a good deal of new Knowledge" (Smyth, VI, 143). Hawkesworth's edition, one of the most important in the history of exploration and discovery, was widely reviewed and read but even in its own day met with some disapproval because its editor, who received more for his official government "hack" work than Fielding did for *Tom Jones*, obviously had done much rewriting, even altering, of the original journals. But Franklin had no access apparently to, say, Cook's own account or, at the time he wrote to Ingenhousz, of Banks's version of the same voyage, both of which Hawkesworth handled as he pleased, changing Cook's natives into more Noble Savages, even Christians, and providing dialogue or drama when needed. Franklin, then, pleased with his friend and thankful for the opportunity to read of places and customs new and fascinating to him, again took the "wrong" side in a travel controversy, since today, with Beaglehole's great Hakluyt edition of Cook,[7] we can quickly see, even partially condone perhaps, Dr. Hawkesworth's methods of editing, which were more or less typical of travel editing of his day, as were those of Smollett and Prévost, for example.

Another controversy Franklin engaged in, while not restricted to travelers or travel editors, was one that involved many travelers of the eighteenth century as well as the scientists and literati who depended on them, that is, the question of whether the plants, animals, and people of the New World were so vigorous, so large, or so long lived as those of the Old World. The French Comte de Buffon (whose pertinent works were published in 1749–88), the Dutch Corneille de Pauw (1770), and the Scot William Robertson (1777) were among the most authoritative spokesmen for the Old World, while the advocates of the New World included not only Thomas Jefferson (1784), but the Frenchman Dom Pernetty (1769), the Scot Lord Monboddo (1773–92), and the Italian Count Carli (1781–83). Well before Jefferson defended the size of American animals by reconstructing a New World mastodon's bones in Paris, Franklin had in London in 1767 received the "tusks and grinders" of a similar mastodon sent him from the Ohio country by George Croghan, his friend and frequent correspondent, the famous Indian trader and interpreter.[8] But at that time the controversy over the size of animals had not yet engrossed educated Europe and Franklin was apparently interested in the question only as a scientist. The argument over whether Americans—native or of European descent—died young, however, had been heated for some time, John Lawson (1709) already having shown to his satisfaction that Americans "live to as great Ages as any of the Europeans." In 1773 the Buffonite de Pauw and the anti-Buffonite Dom Pernetty argued vehemently about the matter, while a few years later the Frenchman Brissot de Warville made a special tour of Massachusetts to inspect the gravestones which the Abbé Robin had in 1781 employed to prove that Americans died early. Then Brissot drew up charts and showed that, contrary to Robin's conclusion, "a man's life is much longer in the United States than in the healthiest country in Europe."[9] In the same year that Franklin turned his mastodon bones over to the Royal Society without, at least in any extant print, using them in the great travel controversy about the New World, he did take a vigorous part in that controversy by publishing in *The London Chronicle* accounts of how people in Pennsylvania were long lived, prefacing his accounts thus:

> I have often heard it remarked, that our Colonies in North America were unhealthy and unfavorable to long life. . . . In opposition to this groundless notion, I here send you two passages from the *Pennsylvania Gazette* . . . and the *New York Gazette* . . . giving an account of the deaths of the first-born of the city of Philadelphia, and of the Province of Pennsylvania. [*Papers*, XIV, 337–39]

Here Franklin, with his moderate, wise approach, was undoubtedly on safer ground than he had been with de Fonte or was to be with Hawkesworth's editing.

So much had he traveled, so well did he know other world travelers, so informed was he in the literature of travel that he even joined a strong tradition by sending advice to a friend preparing for a trip to the Continent. The letter is short because Franklin was busy preparing for his own long journey to Ireland and Scotland, but he took time to suggest that "a good general Rule in travelling foreign Countries, is, to avoid as much as possible all Disputes, and to be content with such Provisions and Cookery, as you meet with in the Inns, so you will have the best the Country affords in the Season . . . and if you attempt to direct the Cookery they will not understand or be able to follow your Orders, and whatever Difficulties you put them to they will be sure to charge you extravagantly for, particularly in Holland" (to Isaac Smith; Smyth, V, 320). In his letter Franklin was doing privately, but in the same way, what travel writers and, especially, editors of collections of voyages had been doing from Gemelli Careri and the Churchill edition early in the century to our own day, when guide books offer detailed advice about hotels and restaurants. Only a short time before, the poet Thomas Gray, after a rather unhappy journey north, had offered similar "Advice to a Friend Travelling in Scotland."[10]

When one remembers how much Franklin traveled and how alive he was to everything around him, one may wonder why he cannot himself be classed among the great eighteenth-century travel writers. Defoe, one of his chief masters in prose style, had written the most important travel book for England, had put together a host of realistic fake travels, and had partially modeled his style on that of William Dampier, called by John Masefield the greatest of travel writers. But then, neither did

Franklin write a long autobiography, carrying it only to his fifty-first year, just to the point when a number of his most intriguing trips were yet to be taken. And, after his early Dogood and Busybody days, he wrote for publication little that was not primarily a scientific paper, a political pamphlet, an official report, or a bagatelle. And even as a scientist he was so busy doing his experiments that he seemed to have little time to write them up, two of the best of these coming, for example, when he was an old man on his last westward crossing of the Atlantic. Likewise, Carl Van Doren adds, "he found it more pleasant to be a philosopher than to write philosophy."[11] In the same fashion, it is easy to see, he was so fond of traveling, of the friends he met and stayed with on the way, of participating, observing, doing that he was not willing to keep diaries or journals or write many long letters about his travels.

Nevertheless, one can find perhaps three passages in his *Autobiography*, select some sixty letters he wrote, combine them with the two journals he kept of his first and last voyages home from Europe, and end with more than a modest volume that could be called "Benjamin Franklin, Eighteenth-Century Travel Writer." Two of the three passages in the *Autobiography* concern Franklin's days on the Indian frontier, first with Braddock, whose stubbornness, vanity, and terrible defeat he described in detail, and second as "General" Franklin in charge of building forts. These accounts are brief, but then they are only part of a brief book, and neither is so detailed—Franklin trusting to a memory of nearly twenty years—that it is to be called great travel reporting. Perhaps the paragraph that best fits the tradition of a Dampier in Central America or a Defoe in Oxford is that one which Franklin begins, "While at Bethlehem, I enquired a little into the practices of the Moravians," and then goes on to tell of his visit to their church, of their music, of the sermon, of their custom of separating the sexes in public, of their pale and unhealthy appearance, and of their marriage customs. The third passage from the *Autobiography* is a longer one that begins with Franklin's departure for New York and his second eastward crossing of the Atlantic and ends with the sentence, "We arrived in London the 27th of July, 1757." Much of this report is taken up with an unfavorable analysis of Lord Loudon's character, "of which *indecision* was one of the strongest features," and of the boring wait at Sandy Hook while Loudon was making up his mind to let the convoy set sail. But then the travel account becomes much more attractive when Franklin tells, first, of how his captain was finally able to outsail all the other ships by moving his forty passengers—and then much of his cargo—aft and, second, how they barely escaped shipwreck near Falmouth.

Franklin's letters are much better as travel accounts even though they are often naturally repetitious because he had to give the same facts to several correspondents, or they are sometimes frustratingly short because of the great pressures brought to bear on him as one of the busiest of men hurrying to get away for a holiday or trying to catch up after returning. And some, perhaps, of his best travel letters have been lost—for example, two to Deborah and one to William Franklin written from Dublin and Glasgow on the second of his two great tours of the United Kingdom.[12] Among the frustratingly brief travel letters—often no more than two sentences in a letter primarily about family or other matters—is one from Williamsburg on March 30 of 1756 when he wrote to Deborah that "Virginia is a pleasant country, now in full spring; the People extreamly obliging and polite" and then simply added that he was planning a week's tour "in the country around," a tour we never hear more about. Again, his 1764 Atlantic crossing, his third eastward one, has almost no word devoted to it in his *Papers*. On the other hand, out of his 1762 westward crossing came a number of relatively fine letters. In one of these, to John Pringle, his scientist friend and travel companion in later years, he wrote (Dec. 1, 1762) only of experiments with water and oil which he conducted on the voyage, an old and perennial passion. But on December 6 and December 7 he sent relatively long letters to Richard Jackson and William Strahan,[13] both back in London, which together provide the kind of attractive information that, say, a Lady Mary Wortley Montague had years before sent from Turkey for her friends at home to read. The best part of these letters is easily Franklin's account of a three-day stopover at Madeira, for he not only gave his impressions of the mountains, the inhabitants, the wheat fields, the fruit trees of the island but was more than usually chatty about how people in the convoy dined back and forth from ship to ship on the slow voyage, of the conviviality, even of how he and others hung Madeira grapes from the cabin ceilings to dry. One of these paragraphs, in fact, was published by Strahan in his *London Chronicle* for March 19–22 (*Papers*, X, 166n) under the caption "Extract of a Letter from Philadelphia, December 7."

One interesting fact, but a natural one, about Franklin's travel letters is that they usually come in bunches, that is, in a short period of time, even on single days. Occasionally, of course, he was hurrying to meet a particular ship's sailing time, say from London to New York or Philadelphia. Often, however, he seemed to be waiting for a few days after returning from a trip in order to catch up on immediate business or recover from the journey before setting aside a half day, an evening, or parts of several days for writing family and friends. There are numerous good examples, but the best of his travel letter days are surely January 13, 1772, when with great pleasure he wrote six different correspondents about the just completed and most extensive land journey he took in the British Isles, that to Ireland and Scotland, and again in July of 1785 when from Southampton he sent off six letters in two days, July 25–26, to describe his journey from Paris and to reassure friends, in almost the same language every time, that he "was not in the least incommoded by the Voyage" from Rouen to the English port.

Among the best of all his travel letters is undoubtedly that one he wrote September 14, 1767, to "Polly" Stevenson (Hewson) after his first visit to Paris. Polly was, of course, a dear friend with whom he could be chatty, gay, even flippant, but the letter displays some of the traveler's wonder and excitement over new places and experiences. Franklin wrote at great length about the Channel crossing, which he, but not others, weathered well, of cheating porters—those in France cheating with more sophistication—of post chaises that leaned too far forward, of the entrance to Paris by the gate St. Denis, of the clean Paris streets and why they were clean, of a gala dinner at Versailles when he and Sir John Pringle ate with the King, Queen, and their two daughters, of the Louvre and the Opéra, of his expenses and new clothes. He even sent a rough diagram of the seating arrangement of the royal family at dinner. "Travelling," he told Polly, "is one Way of lengthening Life, at least in Appearance. It is but a Fortnight since we left London; but the Variety of Scenes we have gone through makes it seem equal to Six Months living in one Place." And then pleasantly he added, "perhaps I have suffered a greater Change too in my own Person than I could have done in Six Years at home. I had not been here Six Days before my Taylor and Peruquier had transformed me into a Frenchman . . . so being in Paris where the Mode is to be sacredly follow'd, I was once very near making Love to my Friend's Wife" (*Papers*, XIV, 250–55). Polly was always one of his favorite correspondents, but never again would Franklin tell her or anyone else so much about a trip or a place he visited.

His two travel journals are, in fact, hardly more attractive than that letter from Paris, although they are much longer and are formal attempts at travel literature. The first, written when he was twenty, is a twenty-seven-page account of his voyage back to America after a year in England (*Papers*, I, 72–79). Almost half of it is concerned with the days he and others spent at Southampton and the Isle of Wight waiting for favorable winds. Like a typical tourist Franklin visited the old Governor's Castle and not only described it but, like an Addison in Italy or a Woodes Rogers in Brazil, dug up a bit of its history. He narrated entertainingly how he helped steal a recalcitrant pilot's boat one night in order to get back to the anchored ship and how the theft backfired. Even more enjoyable is the daily log he kept for much of the voyage, once the Captain received the winds he wanted. For many days dolphins followed the ship and provided excitement as crew and passengers joined in trying to catch them for food, sometimes succeeding, often failing. Other ships were sighted, some passing Franklin's, others sailing east. He told well of the flying fish they saw and of the sharks with their herds of "pilot fish" that sometimes kept him from taking his daily swim alongside the ship. His scientific bent comes through in all this interest in sea fowls and animals but especially in his fascination with the tiny crabs that clung to seaweed he fished out of the ocean one hundred miles from Philadelphia and then put in bottles of salt water to see what would happen after he took them ashore. The most intriguing story in this early journal is of a gambler caught marking two decks of cards and of his trial, which was held somewhat in the tradition, say, of the mock trials witnessed a generation before by Gemelli Careri on a great Spanish galleon in the Pacific when passengers paid for their sins by giving bars of chocolate to the crewmen acting as judge and jury. But the crooked gambler's sentence was not to be so light—he was strung to the mast by a rope tied around his waist until he confessed. What Franklin did not tell, however, is that he was one of those who tied the culprit and strung him up. All and all, this early journal is Franklin's consistently best piece of travel writing.

When he wrote it, Franklin was young, a beginner hoping to record for his future enjoyment—perhaps for posterity—the sights and events he experienced as a far traveler. Not until he was almost sixty years older, in 1785, would he try it again, and by that time the enthusiasm was missing, the thrill of discovery was gone after so many sea voyages and land excursions. In fact, that second journal is merely a fragment of seven pages (Smyth, X, 464–71) that starts ambitiously enough to tell of Franklin's last long journey, that from Paris to Philadelphia, and then fades away when he gets out on the Atlantic. Its real worth lies then in its account of the coach ride to Rouen, of all the hospitality accorded the venerable and popular sage en route, of dinners and parties accepted or necessarily rejected, of the Channel crossing, and of the joyful times he spent with old English friends at Southampton. But then when his ship sailed on July 28 he gave up his journal for two scientific treatises he felt urged to finish, returning to it only during the two days before landing at Philadelphia on September 14. Nevertheless, for an old man of many interests, plagued by the gout, required to be in bed early each night, this last journal is an admirable conclusion for a long life of traveling and writing about traveling.

There is yet one other way in which Franklin was closely related to the great eighteenth-century travel tradition. Not only did he write travel journals and letters and back real voyages of exploration, both with his interest and his money; like all his learned contemporaries he was so widely read in the literature of travel that he knew those books by real travelers like Kalm and Crèvecoeur and Cook as well as those books by fake travelers like his master Defoe and those imaginary voyages such as

Gulliver's Travels or d'Argens' *Jewish Spy*. He was, in other words, well acquainted with pseudotravel literature, an ancient and popular form for romanticists employing local color, for satirists, for Utopians, for deceivers, whether liars or simply hoaxers. As early as the *Dogood Papers,* Franklin as a writer was employing the fictional journey motif. In Dogood No. 1, just as Addison in *Spectator* No. 1 had made a trip to Grand Cairo, the fifteen-year-old Boston author explained that he was born on a ship sailing between Old and New England and that on the same day he was made an orphan when a wave washed his father overboard. Dogood No. 4, another imitation of *The Spectator,* is a travel vision with the author dreaming of a trip across a spacious plain to stately buildings where Idleness and Ignorance reside with want of real learning; the journey ends when the dream traveler learns he is on the campus of Harvard University.

Franklin perpetrated one of his most amusing hoaxes, and a typical one for him, in *The Public Advertiser* in 1765. After writing a letter to that paper on May 10, calling himself "The Spectator" and pretending to be an Englishman dismayed at the lack of veracity exhibited by people sending in information to the newspapers, he responded to his own letter on May 22, this time calling himself "A Traveller." After describing the typical, exaggerating voyager, Franklin defended him by reminding readers of the "innocent Amusement" such a voyager furnishes, of how the public "discuss the Motives to such Voyages, the Probability of their being undertaken. . . . Here we can display our Judgment in Politics, our Knowledge of the Interests [self-interest] of Princes, and our Skill in Geography." Then our correspondent arrived at his point: "But, Sir, I beg leave to say, that all the Articles of News, that seem improbable, are not mere Inventions. Some of them I can assure you, on the Faith of a Traveller, are serious Truths." The serious truths now turn out to be travelers' tales invented to defend the growth of American manufacturing and to counter false facts reported about Franklin's America, all his tales being in the tradition of oversize manatee or snakes, of fictitious birds, of Patagonian giants reported by countless travelers. To destroy the false notion that wool manufacturing would not be feasible in America because its sheep produced too little wool, Franklin gravely insisted that, on the contrary, "the very Tails of the American Sheep are so laden with Wool, that each has a Car or Waggon on four little Wheels to support and keep it from trailing on the Ground." This long "tail" has a long history among travelers. Starting apparently with Herodotus (Book III), who has such long, heavily laden tails on Arabian sheep, the story was repeated by Jean Theneaud, *Le Voyage et itinéraire de oustre mer,* and then in Ramusio's version (1550) of Leo Africanus's *Description of Africa.* Franklin, however, almost surely got it from Rabelais, who in *Gargantua* (Chap. XVI) credits Theneaud for the fact that "a little truck has to be fastened behind the sheep of Syria to bear up their tails, so long and heavy are they." "A Traveller" supported New World silk and iron manufacturing in the same "serious" vein but saved his best tale for last. To demolish the foolish reports, actually appearing in the same *Public Advertiser*, of whale fisheries in the Great Lakes, "A Traveller" explained that cod, a salt water fish, "like other Fish, when attacked by their Enemies, fly into any Water where they think they can be safest." As a result, "Whales, when they have a Mind to eat Cod, pursue them wherever they fly; and . . . the grand leap of the Whale in that Chace up the Fall of Niagara is esteemed by all who have seen it, as one of the finest Spectacles in Nature!" Our "Traveller," obviously well acquainted with America, concluded with a plea for more credulity. This hoax of Franklin's is, of course, only one of the funniest and most famous of many he published. Certain sources for it have been suggested and contemporaneous newspaper pieces have been found that obviously helped to inspire it,[14] but just as obvious is the fact that Franklin's techniques in the hoax are not only those of the travel writer who was notoriously an exaggerator, even a liar, but of the travel editor, or pretended editor, who seriously, or playfully, defended the authenticity of his account. *Gulliver*, filled with marvels and yet with its mock-serious defensive prefatory "Letter to Captain Sympson," was already the product of a long tradition of pseudotravels that included Vairasse, Tyssot, Misson, and Defoe. And every author, or ghost writer, or editor of any one of the many books deriving from George Anson's circumnavigation in the 1740s felt compelled to vouch for the authenticity, the truthfulness, of his version of the voyage. From Lucian to 1765 and beyond, the "traveller" was a liar on the stand facing a hostile courtroom. Franklin knew that well.

Among the greatest of "lying" travelers was the Baron Munchausen, as invented by Rudolph Erich Raspe to amuse mankind and satirize the exploits of real travelers like James "Abysinnian" Bruce. And Franklin knew not only Raspe, whom he met in Hanover in July of 1766, but the even more famous Freiherr von Münchausen, whom he met on the same trip and who was the original for the fictitious teller of marvelous tales. Raspe, one of the eighteenth century's notorious adventurers, was a scholar, linguist, scientist, mining engineer, poet, editor, coin expert, and librarian to the Landgrave of Hesse.[15] Impressed with Franklin he began a correspondence with the great man, even offered to move to America, but instead stole coins placed in his care and had to flee to London about the time Franklin left there in 1775. Horace Walpole, who became his friend and patron, may have had much to do with Raspe's recreation of Münchausen. At any rate, it is a curious fact that Walpole, hardly an admirer of things American, always admired and defended

Raspe's friend Franklin, scornfully suggesting during the heat of the Revolution, for example, that the members of the British cabinet council should go to Franklin in Paris so he could kick them all the way back to London. Again he correctly guessed in 1782, because, he said, no one else was good enough to write it, that Franklin was the author of the gruesome and effective hoax called *Supplement to the Boston Indepen- dent Chronicle.*[16] There is no record that Franklin ever tried to rescue Raspe from any of his illegal acts, but obviously he admired Raspe's genius as a scientist, and just as obviously he and Raspe were brother travel hoaxers.

Much has been said about another "hoax" of Franklin's, the three Indian stories he told in *Remarks Concerning the Savages of North America,* a piece apparently published in Passy in 1784. Over twenty years ago A. O. Aldridge showed beautifully how Franklin wrote this piece by taking elements from other works published in the eighteenth century.[17] What is important here, however, is that the three stories are also all in the best travel-literature tradition. In each of them a wise Indian orator acted as spokesman for the simple life as castigator of the corrupt ways of civilization. One Indian countered the White Man's offer to educate six Indian youths at William and Mary by offering to take twelve youths of European descent "and make *men* of them." Another listened sweetly while a Swedish minister told him of the apple in Eden and of the Christian miracles, but when his own creation myth was angrily rejected as "Fable, Fiction, and Falsehood," the deistic Franklin's "savage" calmly lectured the missionary on the "rules of Common Civil- ity" and urged him to believe that the Indian creation stories were as true as those of the Christian.[18] The third of Franklin's clever Indians is Canasetego, a real Onondaga chieftain whose orations Franklin had him- self printed in Philadelphia in 1744. And the white man he overcame in a kind of debate over Christian business methods is Conrad Weiser, a friend of Franklin and a great Indian scout and interpreter. But the exchange, supposedly told to Franklin by Weiser, like all three of the stories, is surely an invention, if not altogether at least in part. At any rate, while there was a real Canasetego, known by means of Franklin's press and Cadwallader Colden's 1747 reissue, with additions, of his influential *History of the Five Indian Nations.*[19] Canasetego was also a travel-book legend when Franklin used him in 1784, John Shebbeare being only one to employ the name for his Noble Savage hero who in *Lydia* (1755) leaves his golden age environment to sail to England and learn through hard experience of the evil ways of civilization. Further- more, all of these successful savage orators are in the great travel tradi- tion in that each is an example of what should be called the Adario motif after a real Canadian Indian warrior and orator of renown. The real Adario died just in time for the "mendacious" Baron Lahontan to use his name and reputation in a long section of the widely reprinted *Nouveau voyage de M. le baron Lahontan, dans l'Amérique Septentrionale* (1703), a section called "Dialogues curieux entre l'auteur et un sauvage de bon sens qui a voyagé, . . . ," in which Lahontan set himself up as a naive foil to be bested by the wise Indian in a discussion of Christianity and of European government. It was this section, as well as that one telling of the fictitious "Rivière longue," that Lahontan—or his editor Nicholas Gueudeville—expanded to nearly twice its length for the 1705 English edition of his *New Voyage* and that became a commonplace in travel literature, in fiction, and in journalism of the eighteenth century. In fact, not only were there numerous other Adarios—for example, the one invented by another "lying" traveler, the British Thomas Ashe, a hundred years later—but Gilbert Chinard has insisted that every travel writer of the period felt it necessary to include a wise debater like Adario.[20] All three of Franklin's Indians, then—his "educator," the clever Canasetego, and the Noble Savage whose deistic oration was delivered thirty years before it was "translated" into the 1731 Uppsala commencement address— all these are typical examples of one of the thriving travel techniques of Franklin's day.

His triple use of the Adario motif near the end of his life may be the subtlest, and yet most convincing, indication that he was a product of a time when travelers and travel writers were so important, not just for spreading marvelous facts about strange new worlds or inspiring readable pseudotravel books of all kinds but for influencing philosophers such as John Locke, political scientists such as Montesquieu, scientists such as Buffon, or authors of belles lettres such as Defoe, Swift, Prévost, Smollett, Voltaire, and Bernardin de Saint Pierre. In fact, from the time he offered his first feeble prose to the world in the *Dogood Papers* until he ended his life as a seasoned journalist and politician, Franklin was an inveterate traveler, both in the flesh and in the imagination, and he knew well the tradition of the travel writer. As a businessman he backed voyages in the hope of making money and discovering a northern route to China; as a humanitarian he projected another, abortive, voyage to the South Seas; as a scientist he eagerly awaited news of expeditions to the North Pole or befriended Captain Cook; as an inquisitive scholar he read of new customs and lands; as a propagandist for his country he employed the exaggerations common to "lying" travelers; as a political polemicist he argued with the techniques of a tradition created by real and false travelers; as a hoaxer he often joined the ranks of that myriad of hoaxing travelers; and he himself wrote worthwhile travel literature that described places he saw or that narrated in journal form the daily events of voyages he took.

NOTES

1. In Introduction to *Benjamin Franklin: Autobiography and Other Writings* (Boston: Houghton Mifflin, 1949), p. xviii.
2. See letter from Raspe of March 17, 1770, and note by editor in *The Papers of Benjamin Franklin*, ed. Leonard W. Labaree et al. (New Haven and London: Yale University Press, 1959–), XVII, 102 (hereinafter called *Papers*); and Percy G. Adams, "Crèvecoeur and Franklin," *Pennsylvania History*, 14 (October 1957), 273–79.
3. Albert Henry Smyth, ed., *The Writings of Benjamin Franklin* (New York: Macmillan, 1907), IX, 697. Hereinafter called Smyth.
4. See *Papers*, III, 300, 325, 329, 449; IV (see this volume's index); Carl Van Doren, *Benjamin Franklin* (New York: Viking, 1938), p. 197; and Percy G. Adams, "The Case of Swaine versus Drage: An Eighteenth-Century Publishing Mystery Solved," *Essays in History and Literature Presented by Fellows of The Newberry Library to Stanley Pargellis*, ed. Heinz Blum (Chicago: The Newberry Library, 1965), pp. 157–69, which provides numerous pertinent references for the abortive *Argo* expeditions while showing Swaine and Drage to be the same person.
5. For full information about this, one of Franklin's great mistakes, see Bertha Solis-Cohen, who first published the letter and her preface to it as "Benjamin Franklin Defends Northwest Passage Navigation," *Princeton University Library Chronicle*, 19, No. 1 (Autumn 1957), 15–33; Henry R. Wagner, "Apocryphal Voyages to the Northwest Coast of America," *Proceedings of the American Antiquarian Society*, N.S., 41, Part 1 (April 15, 1931), 190–96, who is only one of many to show the impossibility of de Fonte's geography; Percy G. Adams, "Benjamin Franklin's Defense of the de Fonte Hoax," *Princeton University Library Chronicle*, 22, No. 3 (Spring 1961), 133–41; and *Papers*, X, 85–100, the editors of which thoroughly review the entire controversy and Franklin's part in it.
6. Dr. John Hawkesworth, *An Account of the Voyages Undertaken . . . by Commodore Byron, Captain Wallis, and Captain Cook*, 3 vols. (London: W. Strahan & T. Cadell, 1773).
7. Besides *The Journals of Captain James Cook . . .*, 3 vols., ed. J. C. Beaglehole (Cambridge: Published for the Hakluyt Society, 1955–67), with its excellent introduction and notes, one can turn to earlier studies such as H. N. Fairchild, *The Noble Savage* (1928; rpt. New York: Russell, 1955), pp. 104–12.
8. To Croghan, Aug. 5, 1767, *Papers*, XVI, 221. See also *Papers*, XVI, 25–29, for a discussion of these bones, the papers printed about them in the *Philosophical Transactions*, 62, Part 1 (London, 1768), and the philosophical discussions and surmises they gave rise to.
9. For all these travelers and more, see Percy G. Adams, *Travelers and Travel Liars, 1660–1800* (Los Angeles and Berkeley: University of California Press, 1962), pp. 183–85.
10. See J. Bennett Nolan, *Benjamin Franklin in Scotland and Ireland*

(Philadelphia: University of Pennsylvania Press, 1956), p. 41.

11. Van Doren, p. 292.

12. Nolan (see note 10), in fact, in his very readable attempted reconstruction of these two trips, one in 1759, one in 1771–72, was forced to depend for his information far more on surmises and on records kept by other people than on Franklin's own words.

13. *Papers*, X, 163, 166–67. See Nolan, pp. 132–39, for information about Franklin's close friend and associate, Richard Jackson, who accompanied him on the second Scottish tour and who was well known to Dr. Johnson. Strahan, Franklin's lifelong printer friend, needs no introduction here.

14. See especially Verner W. Crane, *Benjamin Franklin's Letters to the Press 1758–1775* (Chapel Hill: University of North Carolina Press, 1950), and, for the essay and helpful notes, *Papers*, XII, 132–35.

15. For more on Raspe and his connections with Walpole and Bruce, see Adams, *Travelers*, pp. 216–18.

16. See especially Van Doren, pp. 572, 560, 673.

17. Aldridge, "Franklin's Deistical Indians," *Proceedings of the American Philosophical Society*, 94 (1950), 398–410. Aldridge also treats the hoax, almost surely Franklin's, called "The Captivity of William Henry in 1755." This piece, printed and discussed by the editors of the *Papers*, XV, 145–57, while related to travel literature is more in the tradition of Indian captivities and burlesque Indian myths. It is, of course, another example of Franklin's (or somebody's) use of the Adario motif in that the physiocrat economic system of "Henry's" Indians is permitted to win over the rival mercantilist system. It is interesting that as a possible author of this entertaining story the editors of the *Papers* offer the elder Reinhold Forster, who went on Cook's second voyage and wrote a two-volume account of that voyage. But a study of Forster's many works, and especially of his account of Cook's explorations, uncovers nothing that would lead one to believe that he was capable of such a hoax.

18. Aldridge believed in 1950 that the real origin of this story was a graduation address published in Sweden in 1731 that retold an experience which happened in Canada in 1698 and was then retold in Sweden in 1714. To Aldridge's information about four eighteenth-century uses of the Swedish minister, one can add at least three others—*The London Magazine* of 1760, *The Scot's Magazine* of 1761, and *The Philadelphia Magazine* of 1789—in each case the printing of the story eliciting letters with suggestions about how a Christian might best answer the wise Indian. See Benjamin Bissell, *The American Indian in English Literature of the Eighteenth Century* (1925; rpt. Hamden, Conn.: Archon Books, 1968), p. 75, and the note after this one.

19. Colden's *History* was first published in New York in 1727, reissued in London in 1747 and 1755; the most recent issue is that in Ithaca by the Cornell University Press in 1958. From his friend Colden (see the edition published in New York in 1902, New Amsterdam Book Co., I, 188), Franklin could have taken the first half of one of his three stories in the *Remarks*, that in which the Virginia citizens offer to educate Indian youths, although it is to be found also in "A Treaty . . . in the Town of Lancaster," . . . which Franklin's own press had printed (see Carl Van Doren and Julian P. Boyd, eds., *Indian Treaties Printed by Benjamin Franklin 1736–1762* [Philadelphia: Historical Society of Philadelphia, 1938], p. 76). The Indian rebuttal is obviously Franklin's invention.

20. See Gilbert Chinard, *L'Amérique et le rêve exotique* (1913; rpt. Paris:

E. Droz, 1934), p. 170. For more on the Adario tradition, see Geoffroy Atkinson, *The Extraordinary Voyage in French Literature from 1700 to 1720* (Paris: Champion, 1922), pp. 31–33; and Adams, *Travelers,* pp. 199–201, 230. There were, of course, such wise primitives reported before Adario, as in the case of Baltasar Gracian's Andrenio (see Atkinson) and, even earlier, Jean de Léry's Tupinamba dialogue of 1578 as found in Léry's *Histoire d'un voyage faict en la terre du Bresil . . .* , 2nd ed. (Paris: Antoine Chuppin, 1580), chap. 20. For the Tupinamba "Adario," who was unknown to me, I am indebted to William C. Sturtevant, general editor, *Handbook of North American Indians.* It was Lahontan, however, friend of Leibnitz and a real influence on writers from Swift to the Encyclopédistes, who gave the tradition its greatest impetus.

PART II

Franklin as Writer

P. M. Zall

🦋 A Portrait of the
Autobiographer as an Old Artificer

The manuscript of Franklin's *Autobiography* lies open to public view twenty-seven hours a week, eleven months of the year, at the center of the magnificent treasures in the Huntington Library. There visitors from all over the world file silently by the Ellesmere Chaucer, the Gutenberg Bible, the Shakespeare First Folio, then swarm around the *Autobiography*. These happy legions thus see Franklin more plainly than practicing critics who rely solely on "standard texts," because the *Autobiography* has never been edited half so thoroughly as any of its distinguished neighbors. The transcription of the manuscript for Max Farrand's Parallel Text Edition gave us only a sampling of the many changes in wording or of the cancellations on every one of the 230 pages, and seldom indicated that many passages crucial to plot, characterization, and theme had come about through cunning craftsmanship rather than spontaneous composition. Then the Yale edition simplified Farrand's textual apparatus "for the convenience of readers,"[1] and placed unwary critics at two removes from the manuscript, thus subjecting them to the needless risk of slicing away at Franklin's art with a speckled Occam's razor.

The wonder is that, even without the manuscript, they have done so well in intuiting the art behind the *Autobiography*. The seminal study by A. Owen Aldridge proposed its psychological unity, another by Robert F. Sayre disclosed the rhetorical structure that binds the two points of view, of the man written about and the man writing. A succeeding generation represented by John Griffith and James A. Sappenfield has been applying finely honed tools of rhetorical analysis to uncover an internal arrangement of elements making up a psychic substructure. While all concur that the formal structure of the whole may be (in Aldridge's phrase) "total disaster,"[2] that of Part One is worthy the keenest analyses we can apply. This consensus is supported by the manuscript. There, clearly visible to the eye unaided by ultraviolet lamps or magnifying lenses, certain physical features reflect rhetorical strategies of a remarkably high order. They are the more remarkable because unexpected, and they are unexpected because obscured in the standard texts that have incorporated them silently "for the convenience of readers." It might be useful then to describe the obvious physical features that tell us much about the way in which Franklin shaped the plot, characters, and theme of Part One.

The manuscript is entirely in Franklin's hand, and we can tell from folds in the paper and from the penmanship that he composed it in such a way as to make allowances for later alterations. The sheet rather than the page was his unit of composition, and most of the alterations seem to have been made on each sheet as it was completed. He started with a sheet about 16 x 13 inches, folded it lengthways to make four pages, then folded again to form a writing surface about 4 x 13 inches. Unfolded, each page would thus consist of two columns of equivalent width, one for composing, the other for revising. Two hundred of the manuscript's 230 pages contain interpolated words or passages in the columns left blank to receive them.

It is truly too bad that no printed text describes the extent of these interpolations. Their appearance alone evokes the analogy of a wrought iron gate, with dozens of incidents spiraling down the margins, some extending to 67 lines, more than 600 words, over two pages translated into printed text, revealing an ingenuity in structural fabrication we ought to have suspected from the Ben Franklin whose ancestors followed "the Smith's Business" and who delighted in constructing "little Machines" for his experiments while the intention of making them was "fresh and warm" in his mind (ms. pp. 9–10; Y. p. 57).[3]

The manuscript itself seems fresh and warm from his mind, with its false starts and crossings out, over, above, and below the lines, corrections slipped in as the quill forged ahead swift as thought, sometimes not lifting long enough to leave space between words. It would be little short of marvelous if he worked this way without some kind of preconceived design in view, something more useful than the topical outline now at the Morgan Library, with its emphases distorted and its sequence breaking down midway in Part One. The physical appearance of the manuscript provides a better clue to that design in Part One at least, where even the seemingly chaotic interpolations were fabricated in the heat of composition and not, as we might suppose, a dozen years later in the cool of more tranquil recollection. All but a very few sustain the air of fresh improvisation that characterizes the tone of Part One and thus makes them virtually indistinguishable in a printed text that does not point them out as interpolated passages.

Part One is unique in having every page and every sheet numbered. It would seem that Franklin's practice through the first eight sheets (Y. pp. 43–79) was to complete a sheet, plus or minus a paragraph, and then return to review and revise what he had written before forging ahead. Over the next four sheets (Y. pp. 79–93), perhaps from press of time, he wrote in units of half-sheets, or two pages. Thereafter he would generally compose in sheets again, but now beginning with third rather than first pages, any of which, as right-hand pages, lent themselves conveniently to beginning new thoughts and adding afterthoughts in the main body of the text. This invitation to interpolation led to the disruption of logical continuity that some readers find disturbing. But seeing how he worked can help us to understand that he knew where he was going.

For instance, taking the sheet as his basic structural unit, we can see that Franklin constructed Part One in three divisions of equal length, seven-and-a-half sheets each. The correspondence between length and narrative substance is too close to be mere coincidence, since the first division covers the initial trip to Philadelphia (Y. pp. 43–75); the second includes the entire London episode, from its initial proposal through the protagonist's return (Y. pp. 75–106); and the third covers the remainder (Y. pp. 106–131). There are other indications of using the sheet for designing a symmetrical structure. We have a half-sheet-long discourse on the abuse of language in the first division (Y. p. 65) balancing a half-sheet-long discourse on the abuse of faith in the third division (Y. p. 113), both including quotations from Pope (in the latter called "Dryden"); and these have as a pivot the recollection about eating fish that leads to the axiom, "So convenient a thing it is to be a *reasonable Creature,* since it enables one to find or make a Reason for every thing one has a mind to do" (ms. p. 43; Y. p. 88)—on the abuse of reason. Even in the Yale edition, this thematic fulcrum appears in the physical center of Part One. Fantastic as this juggling may seem, it would be second nature to the Franklin who delighted in "making magic Squares, or Circles" (Y. p. 197n.). But to pursue such structural feats further would take us beyond our present scope. It is enough now to see that they reflect a conscious symmetry in structural design.

Printed texts obscure this symmetry because they silently incor-

porate the long interpolations that conflate the substance of individual
sheets. The most extensive instance is the initial interpolation to pages 1
and 2 of the manuscript, which in the Yale edition runs from the phrase,
"and the Journey I took for that purpose" on page 43 down through the
first paragraph on page 45, concluding "whose Power it is to bless to us
even our Afflictions." Another conflation, in the middle of Part One, is the
hilarious episode in which Keimer is conned into a vegetable diet and
almost dies of vexation. The whole episode is a columnar interpolation to
the main text that had first read: "Keimer & I liv'd on a pretty good
Footing & agreed tolerably well: for he suspected nothing of my Setting
up. Hearing me talk of that Mode of Living, he said he would try it if I
would keep him Company. I did so for three Months.— (ms. p. 43; Y. pp.
88, 89). There are a half-dozen other conflations of this kind: Collins,
refusing to row the boat, is made to swim home. Franklin, printing his
free-thinking pamphlet, obtains entry to London club life. Through teach-
ing Wygate to swim, he expands his circle of acquaintance still further.
Three of these long columnar interpolations provide character sketches—
of his maternal grandfather, Peter Folger, of the nameless London nun,
and of the Philadelphia croaker, Samuel Mickle.

    This kind of interpolation has a substantive as opposed to a stylis-
tic function, where the purpose is to revise for tone or precision. Most
often, stylistic interpolations appear as interlinear insertions or tacked on
at line- or paragraph-end. One sentence, for instance, originally read: "I
found I wanted a *Copia Verborum* . . ." (ms. p. 13; Y. p. 62). The Latin
was then translated—"a Stock of Words or a Readiness in finding & Using
what I had,"—which in turn was revised to read: "in recollecting & Using
them"—all between two lines of the main text. The substantive interpolations are frequently squeezed into the main text, but commonly appear
in the margins left blank to receive them, where it is easy to follow
Franklin as he manipulates them for purposes of unity, emphasis, or
coherence, and—most remarkably—for a new point of view.

    At rough count, there are about sixty interpolations of this kind
in Part One alone. Of that number perhaps one-quarter consist of
authorial comments, another quarter refer to characters and the other
half bear upon the action. Alas, few lend themselves to easy theories
about when they were added. Even with the color of ink and quality of
penmanship as indicators, we can assign only a vague date of "about
1771," which would mean during the summer of 1771 when he composed
Part One in England, up to the fall of 1775 when he returned to Philadelphia and would have had little time for composing memoirs. The penmanship remains uniform throughout Part One, offering little help to dating,
and so we are left with such slippery clues as the breadth of a quill point,
the width of a gap between lines or words, or the correspondences be-

tween substance and style reflected in verbal echoes. But even within these limitations, we can see two patterns of interpolation appear so regularly that they can illustrate the way Franklin worked:

The more common pattern consists of insertions made closely after completing a sentence or a sheet. Subsequent allusions in the main body of the text incorporate the substance of an earlier interpolation, making it easy to distinguish between chicken and egg. Thus, Miss Read first sees her husband munching on a roll in Market Street in an interpolated passage on the blank column of ms. page 28, at the end of sheet 7. Then near the end of the next sheet, the main text alludes to that scene when speaking of his "more respectable Appearance in the Eyes of Miss Read" (ms. p. 32; Y. p. 79). The other pattern consists of insertions composed after the bulk of Part One had been completed. The clearest example is a series of five brief passages on his "errata" pointing out instances of moral mistakes made in his wayward youth.

These passages seem so closely connected they could have been written at the same time, clearly after the manuscript had been completed to the end of page 85. They are brief enough to list in order of their appearance:

1. With respect to taking advantage of his brother in black-mailing him with his new "Indenture," marginally on page 22—"and this I therefore reckon one of the first Errata of my Life . . ." (Y. p. 70).

2. With respect to lending Vernon's money, interlinearly on page 40—"The Breaking into this Money of Vernon's was one of the first great Errata of my Life" (Y. p. 86).

3. On sending the letter to Miss Read virtually breaking their engagement, marginally on page 51—"This was <one> ↑another↓ of the great Errata of my Life, which I should wish to correct <in Living a second Edition. Living> if I were to live it over again" (Y. p. 96).

4. Appended to the interpolation about his freethinking pamphlet, which itself appears marginally just below the previous passage on page 51—"<The> ↑My↓ printing this Pamphlet was another Erratum" (Y. p. 96).

5. On taking familiarities with Mrs. T., marginally on page 53—"(another Erratum)" (Y. p. 99).

Along with these are two others, both added at ends of paragraphs, pointing out that he eventually corrected the two "great Errata" at least:

6. After saying he paid off Vernon as soon as he was able—"So that Erratum was in some degree corrected" (ms. p. 76; Y. p. 122).

7. After concluding, "We throve together, and have ever mutually endeavour'd to make each other happy,"—"Thus I corrected that great *Erratum* as well as I could" (ms. p. 85; Y. p. 129).

The entire series seems to have been added in order to support the moral purpose enunciated in the two-column-long interpolation to the very first page of the manuscript. Like the initial interpolation, the errata series shifts the point of view from that of a chronicler to that of a garrulous pater familias. But where the errata series seems to have been inserted at one sitting, the initial interpolation seems to have been composed in three stages, or at least in three segments. The first, speaking of the purpose in writing the work, may have been composed quite early, possibly after the first sheet and the paragraph that concludes, "all grew up to be Men & Women, and married" (Y. p. 51). The second, commenting on the chances of reliving one's life and correcting one's faults along with the calculated risk of appearing vain, seems a separate entity—from the phrase "fit to be imitated" (Y. p. 43) down through "it would not be quite absurd if a Man were to thank God for his Vanity among the other Comforts of Life" (Y. p. 44). The third is distinctively separated—as a separate paragraph and with different penmanship, down to the concluding clause, "in whose Power it is to bless to us even our Afflictions" (Y. p. 45).

My best guess is that the second segment was inserted after Franklin had composed the main text through his marriage (ms. p. 85; Y. p. 129). Then he could have worked quickly through the document inserting the "errata" passages in their proper places—working so quickly in fact that he overlooked one spot where such a passage would have been appropriate: On ms. page 68 (Y. p. 114) he adds an interpolation about his conduct toward Vernon and Miss Read "which at Times gave me great Trouble," but says nothing about "errata." I suspect that at this point he was attracted to a different theme that would lead eventually to adding the third segment of his initial interpolation.

The passage about Vernon and Miss Read is inserted into a long, two-page discussion of his "then State of Mind" appearing on ms. pages 68–70 (Y. pp. 113–15), where it serves as a gloss on the protagonist's moral development. While there are links to the "errata" passages, there are even firmer links with the first segment of the initial interpolation, beginning in virtually the same way: "It may be well to let you know the then State of my Mind, with regard to my Principles and Morals, that you may see how far those influenc'd the Future Events of my Life." And the passage about Vernon and Miss Read concludes with terms that appear in the concluding segment of the first interpolation—"kind hand of Providence" (cf. "kind Providence" on ms. page 2).

It is conceivable, then, that the third segment of the opening interpolation was composed hard upon completing the discourse on ms. pages 68–70. If so, it gave Franklin a chance to establish the irony in the gap between a protagonist who has yet to acquire the faith so fervently expressed in the opening segment by the supposedly garrulous old man:

"I desire with all Humility to acknowledge, that I ↑<firmly believe>↓ owe the mention'd Happiness of my past Life to his kind Providence. . . ." On ms. page 70 that faith is hedged with correlatives as the discourse speaks of having been preserved from "*willful* gross Immorality ↑or Injustice↓" in a godless youth by an innate moral sense "with the kind hand of Providence, or some guardian Angel, or ↑accidental↓ favourable Circumstances & Situations, or all together" (Y. p. 115). Our protagonist there prides himself on having learned wisdom—"that *Truth, Sincerity,* & *Integrity* in Dealings between Man & Man, were of the utmost Importance to the Felicity of Life . . .(ms. p. 69; Y. p. 114). In view of the interpolation on ms. page 2, he has still much to learn. Perhaps the intent is to portray the autobiographer as a *young* man, young in moral development as in years, and quite distinct from the bemused old man now meditating upon his growth.

Besides imposing a new point of view, the interpolations throughout Part One also served purposes of characterization. The knowledge our protagonist has gained in his godless youth must have yielded some good, for no "errata" appear after the discourse on his "then State of Mind." In an interpolated gloss on "wilful" there, he distinguishes, "the Instances I have mentioned, had something of *Necessity* in them, from my Youth, Inexperience, & the Knavery of others." The distinction is a wise one, for he is referring to the "knavery" of Collins, Ralph, and Keith and also to the interpolated mention of his own knavery to Vernon and Miss Read. The others may have preyed upon him, but the meanness to Miss Read at least had been a fault all his own. To "Youth" he could attribute his having fled his brother's printshop, and to "Inexperience" all the others, even the abortive rape of Mrs. T.—for an interpolated phrase at that regrettable scene adds that he was then "under no Religious Restraints" (ms. p. 53; Y. p. 99). It may be that time can cure both youth and inexperience, but here there is a distinction between growing old and growing up. The difference lies in the distinction between "Necessity" and individual responsibility.

The development of this mature distinction in the youth's mind is nicely reflected in another series of a half-dozen interpolations touching upon his courtship of the unfortunate Miss Read. That courtship properly begins in the middle of Part One where the manuscript first read cooly: "I had made some Courtship during this time to <my> Miss Read, <and> but as I was about to take a voyage, and we were both very young, ↑only a little above 18↓ it was thought most prudent by her Mother . . . to prevent our going too far at present, as a Marriage if it was to take place . . . would be more convenient after my Return, when I should be as I . . . expected set up in my Business. Perhaps too she thought my Expectations not so well founded as I imagined them to be" (ms. p. 43;

Y. p. 89). In the middle of the first sentence, an interpolation injects at least a little feeling into the suitor: "I had a great Respect & Affection for her, and had some Reason to believe she had the same for me."

As the plot is played out, he gradually forgets Miss Read among the fleshpots of London, writing only one letter, "& that was to <prevent her> let her know I was not likely soon to return"—marked as "↑another↓ of the great Errata" (ms. p. 51; Y., p. 96). Returning to Philadelphia he sees Keith avoiding him on the street and now muses, "I should have been as much asham'd at seeing Miss Read" had not her relatives persuaded her to wed another in the meantime, "despairing ↑with Reason↓ of my Return"—and an interpolation adds the twinge of conscience, "after the Receipt of my Letter" (ms. p. 59; Y. p. 107). Other interpolations at this point stress that she had parted from her husband because he was a scoundrel, said to have another wife; he had run away after wasting her dowry. The later passages that reveal the outcome of the courtship pick up some of the material deleted here with the apparent aim of strengthening the conflict there, but even there the interpolations emphasize not only what happened but how the protagonist felt: One pertinent passage first read, "I pity'd poor Miss Read's unfortunate Situation," and Franklin interpolated a pathetic expansion: "who was generally dejected, seldom chearful, and avoided Company" (ms. p. 85; Y. p. 129).

This may seem to some a fumbling attempt at superimposing a traditional romantic plot—with parental prudence isolating the young lover, the cruel letter, the guilt, the ultimate obstacle in the husband whose fate is in doubt, and the final union. But besides adding an element of pathos, the interpolations about Miss Read stress a developing emotional maturity in the lover who, at the end, ventures on the match with a prudence to match his mother-in-law's. And, as a serendipitous bonus, they dramatize the mental motion of the narrator himself as he tries to convey not just the experience but the quality of the experience evoked by his recollection.

If the attempt at evoking this double vision seems too sophisticated for a mere and hasty memoir, consider the way other interpolations point to novelistic devices that help support development of character and theme. A clear example is the recurring of the words "ingenious" or "sensible" to make qualitative comments on almost all characters, major and minor—and yet, notably, not in association with Miss Read or Mr. Denham, the two for whom he apparently feels deeply. Uncle Benjamin is "ingenious" and so is Mr. Matthew Adams. Dr. Brown is "ingenious, but much of an Unbeliever." Brother James in Boston has ingenious friends and so has Franklin in Philadelphia. Watson is "pious, sensible, of Great Integrity"; Maugridge, "solid, sensible"; Meredith, "honest, sensible"; while Osborne, originally only "candid and frank" is made "sensible" by an interpolated term. His Burlington friend Decow, on the other hand, was at first "shrewd, sensible" before "sensible" was changed to "sagacious." Franklin's "sensible" refers to intrinsic qualities of good sense, while "ingenious" seems to refer to acquired talents or skills. Breintnal, for instance, is said to have been "very ingenious in many little Nicknackeries," but he also carried on "sensible Conversation." It would seem then that the combination seen in this favorite friend would be desirable. Yet in meditating upon Keith's villanies, the narrator calls him "an ingenious, sensible man" with all his faults, as if the combination in itself was insufficient to make a good man. Closer to a model would be the personality of William Coleman, who combined "the coolest clearest Head, the best Heart, and the exactest Morals, of almost any Man I ever met with" and whose friendship lasted forty years (ms. p. 72; Y. p. 118).

The term "almost" leaves room for Mr. Denham, the Quaker merchant, who appears shortly after the pivotal midpoint of Part One, a half-dozen pages after the narrator says of Governor Keith, "I believ'd him one of the best Men in the World" (ms. p. 41; Y. p. 87). But there also we are prepared for his appearance by the ruminative passage: "I had hitherto kept the Proposition ↑of my setting up↓ a Secret in Philadelphia, & I still kept ↑it↓. Had it been known that I depended on the Governor, probably some Friend ↑that knew him better↓ would have advis'd me not to rely on him. . . ." That friend, Denham, appears on page 50, where he "let me into Keith's Character" (Y. p. 94), and thereafter sees him through the second division of Part One with paternal but unobtrusive care: "He counsell'd me as a Father, <& seem'd to> having a sincere Regard for me: I <lo> respected & lov'd him" (ms. p. 60; Y. p. 107).

In contrast, his "ingenious" father is hardly treated with respect or affection after the opening sheets. Though "ingenious," his "great Excellence lay in a sound Understanding, and solid Judgment in prudential Matters" (ms. p. 7; Y. p. 54). But there is irony in the term "prudential." For in the manuscript, page 36, when he rejects Keith's offer to set up the boy in business as improper, a cancelled passage had said his objection was based on prudence: "He had advanc'd too much already to my Brother James" (Y. p. 82n.). This gap between explicit and implicit value is seen also in the advice his father offers, telling him in effect to keep on doing what he has been doing. This advice "was all I could obtain," except (an interpolation tactfully adds) "some small Gifts as Tokens of his & my Mother's Love" (ms. p. 37; Y. p. 83). There is poignant contrast here with a later statement about the small legacy Denham leaves him in the imprudently nuncupative will, "as a Token of his <Regard good Will to> ↑Kindness↓ for me, and he left me once more to the wide World" (ms. pp. 60–61; Y. p. 107). Then, following his father's advice, he does achieve a kind of success through impressing

customers with the *appearance* of industry, as in pushing paper through
the streets in a wheelbarrow—as if the appearance of industry were its
substance—or public "esteem" were the essence of integrity. This con-
trasts sharply with Denham's way of doing business. At one time a bank-
rupt, he recouped his losses in America through "a close Application" in
a few years, then paid off "his old Creditors" by thanking them and surprising each with "the full Amount of the ↑unpaid↓ Remainder <.->
[with Interest.]" (ms. p. 57; Y. 105). The interpolations to that passage
are significant in view of the way the protagonist later specifies how he
repaid Vernon: "I paid the <Principle> Principal with Interest & many
Thanks.–" (ms. p. 76; Y. p. 122). The influence of Denham seems to
extend over the entire third division of Part One, and it is doubtless from
him that he became convinced "that *Truth, Sincerity & Integrity* in Dealings between Man & Man, were of the utmost Importance to the Felicity
of Life"—a conviction that he describes with the good Quaker term,
"Persuasion" (ms. p. 69; Y. p. 115). Thus Denham's leaving him "once
more to the wide World" is in the physical rather than spiritual sense. It
must be thanks to Denham's influence that hereafter are no more "errata";
only a series of choices reasonably resolved.

He had been faced with many choices earlier, at least three crucial
choices in the two earlier divisions of Part One. In the first, they seemed
guided by youthful impulse; and in the second, influenced by inexperience
or the knavery of others. But note that even his early decision to leave
Boston involves a "reasoning" process. It is determined not by his brother's
meanness, but in consideration of his own liberty and safety. The pertinent passage is a columnar interpolation to page 22, beginning "and I
was the rather inclin'd to leave Boston," and concluding "it was likely I
might [if I stay'd] ↑soon↓ bring myself into Scrapes; and [farther that]
my indiscrete Disputations about Religion <had made me> began to
make me pointed at with Horror by good People, as an Infidel or Atheist;
I determin'd <on the> [on the] Point" (Y. p. 71). This determination
easily suppresses his conscience ("It was not fair in me")—a clear illustration of the pivotal axiom: "So convenient a thing it is to be a *reasonable
Creature,* since it enables one to find or make a Reason for every thing
one has a mind to do."

In the course of the second division, he learns to be more circum-
spect in dealing with such knaves as Keith or such tempters as Collins and
Ralph. Thus when Wygate proposes that they tour Europe together, the
protagonist consults his friend Denham who dissuades him from it, "ad-
vising me to think only of return^g to Pensilvania [.–], which he was now
about to do" (ms. p. 57; Y. p. 104). But, while waiting for the ship home,
he entertains Sir William Wyndham's proposition that he stay and teach

his sons to swim, an offer rejected because he had already agreed to go with Denham as his clerk: the boys "were not yet come to Town and <I expected> my Stay was uncertain." It strikes him, though, "that had the Overture been sooner made me, probably I should not so soon have returned to America" (ms. p. 59; Y. p. 106). An interpolation makes plain that in returning with Denham he would be not only working for a lower wage but passing up this opportunity to make "a good deal of Money."

The crucial decisions in the third division are scrupulous also, and all the more significant in now being made without the advice of Denham. His brother-in-law Holmes advises him to leave grocery clerking and return to printing, but he holds out until lack of employment in the grocery business drives him to Keimer. Keimer had been trying to entice his return by holding out great wages, but the protagonist had heard "a bad Character of him in London . . . & was not fond of having any more to do with him" (ms. p. 61; Y. p. 108). Thus his subsequent "break" with Keimer was less impulsive than it was a recognition of his own connivance in Keimer's knavery against him. Emphasizing the difference between this and the earlier break with his brother, an interpolation has Keimer "expressing a Wish that he had not been oblig'd to <it;> so long a Warning" (ms. p. 64; Y. p. 111). The ensuing reconciliation is a calculated expedient on both sides—Keimer's to obtain needed skills, and his to tide him over the time required to set up shop with Meredith. But there is no question about the decision that goes counter to his friends' advice that he dissolve the partnership with Meredith, whose idling, drinking, and then failure to provide funding threatens ruin: "I told them I could not propose <such a thing> ↑a Separation↓ while any Prospect remain'd of the Merediths fulfilling their Part of our Agreement." And an interpolation adds: "Because I thought my self under great Obligations to them for what they had done & would do if they could" (ms. p. 77; Y. p. 122)—a clear illustration of *"Truth, Sincerity & Integrity* in Dealings between Man & Man."

His maturity in these respects is further emphasized when he is faced by Godfrey's relatives with the choice of taking their daughter without a dowry or not having her at all. An interpolation emphasizes that "the Girl being in herself very deserving" was attractive to him. But when her parents raise their prudent objections about his prospects, he weighs their motives and finds them wanting in truth, sincerity, and integrity: "Whether this was ↑a↓ real ↑Change of Sentiment,↓ or only Artifice, on a Supposition of our being too far engag'd in Affection to retract . . . I know not" (ms. pp. 83–84; Y. pp. 127–28). But he suspected the worst and broke off the match, despite his inclination for the girl. Thus by the time he must decide about marrying Miss Read he comes equipped with a clear head and exact ethical standards, capable of nicely balancing principle and inclination, no longer merely a reasonable creature who can rationalize everything he has a mind to do.

He also has a hungry heart. This is made clear as, after prospecting fruitlessly for a wife he could love, he muses in despair: "I was not to expect Money with a Wife unless with such a one, as I should not otherwise think agreable" (ms. p. 84; Y. p. 128). Now he would not repress inclination for the sake of prudence; still there is another factor to take into account. Earlier, on page 70, a statement had been deleted from the passage flattering himself on having escaped "gross Immorality": "Some foolish Intrigues with low Women excepted, which from the Expence were rather more <inconvenient> prejudicial to me than to them." Fourteen pages later that statement is both transposed and transformed in the main text: "In the mean time, that hard-to-be-govern'd Passion of Youth, *[had]* hurried me frequently into Intrigues with <such> low Women <as> ↑that↓ fell in my Way, which were attended with some Expence & ↑great↓ Inconvenience, besides a continual Risque to my Health by a Distemper which of all Things I dreaded, tho' by great good Luck I escaped it."

But it is a stronger force than either prudence or prophylaxis that moves the match with Miss Read. The ensuing paragraph originally attributed the Read family's regard for him to the fact that the youngest daughter had married his old friend Watson ("and had some Regard for me on his Account"). This passage was changed so that their regard existed from the time of his first lodging with them—thus serving the function of a reprise. For the next statement says that they turned to him for consultation and service, just as, generations earlier, friends had turned to his father, and more recently he had turned to Denham, and—even more pertinent—Mrs. T. had turned to him. It is now that he pities Miss Read, "who was generally dejected, seldom chearful, and avoided Company," a description contrasting with that of Mrs. T., who had been "sensible & lively, <an> and of most pleasing Conversation" (ms. p. 51; Y. p. 98).

From that interpolated pity, his decision begins to take shape in the crucible of his conscience, somewhat colored by the "Obligations" he had felt toward the Merediths. This decision has two elements—his inconsiderate neglect and (emphasized in an interpolation subsequently canceled) the foolish letter that had led to her fruitless marriage and miserable dejection. Another interpolation adds the catalyst: "Our mutual Affection was revived." And in the boldness of their new bond, they withstand the manifold "great Objections" to a prudent match: Another early cancellation appears, to tease about her husband possibly having another wife, or possibly being dead—but, if dead, their being responsible for his debts. Then it is with a pregnant verb that we are told they "ventur'd . . . over all these difficulties," while another interpolation reassures us of that venture's success: "prov'd a good Wife" is deleted in favor of "prov'd a good & faithful Helpmate."

This union of head, heart, and conscience is sealed by another interpolation that absorbs the color of his "Obligations" to the Merediths "for what they had done & would do if they could." As earlier interpolations had developed the point of view, action, and characters, so it is the last interpolation on this page that tops off the theme: "Thus I corrected that great *Erratum* as well as I could." The young man has come to see both the power of prudence and the glory of conscience. We can now rest assured that he will go forth to forge in the smithy of his craft the uncreated conscience of his nation.

NOTES

1. *The Autobiography of Benjamin Franklin,* ed. Leonard W. Labaree et al. (New Haven: Yale University Press, 1964), p. 39.

2. A. Owen Aldridge, "Form and Substance in Franklin's Autobiography," *Essays on American Literature,* ed. Clarence Gohdes (Durham: University of North Carolina Press, 1967), p. 48; John Griffith, "The Rhetoric of Franklin's Autobiography," *Criticism,* 13 (1971), 81; James A. Sappenfield, *A Sweet Instruction* (Carbondale: Southern Illinois University Press, 1973), p. 182; and Robert F. Sayre, *The Examined Self* (Princeton: Princeton University Press, 1964), p. 18.

Page references are to the manuscript (ms.) in the Henry E. Huntington Library, HM 9999, and the comparable passages in the Yale edition of the *Autobiography.* In the quotations, made possible through the permission of the Librarian, the Huntington Library, deletions are indicated by < >; interlinear insertions by ↑ ↓; and columnar insertions by [ ].

David L. Parker   ❧ **From Sound Believer**

to Practical Preparationist: Some Puritan

Harmonics in Franklin's *Autobiography*

By now the portrait of Benjamin Franklin as a desanctified pragmatic Puritan, a secular preacher of utilitarian virtue, has come to merit at least passing mention in most commentaries on the *Autobiography*. Generally noted in this connection have been Franklin's regard for Cotton Mather's *Essays to Do Good*, his stress on diligence in a calling, his preoccupation with testing moral principles in everyday experience, his introspective cast of mind, and his emphasis on the importance of upright conduct.[1] Larzer Ziff has summarized what seems to be the prevailing view of the relation between Franklin's pragmatism and Puritan piety:

> Benjamin Franklin, the runaway heir of the Puritan intellectual tradition, accepted the habits on which it so insisted but measured the value of those habits in terms of their ability to achieve beneficial results rather than in terms of what they revealed about the state of sanctification of the doer. He accepted his inherited zeal for knowledge, but he applied it to the good and the useful rather than to the holy and the absolutely true.[2]

My intent is not so much to modify this view of Franklin as to amplify it through a more particular consideration of Franklin's "bold and arduous Project of arriving at moral Perfection"[3] in comparison to certain Puritan ideals. More specifically, I intend to compare this "project" to the sequentially staged conversion process outlined by Puritan minis-

67

ters, for Franklin's efforts proceed at least loosely by similar stages. Furthermore, while his initial optimistic confidence in his ability to achieve the desired results perhaps reflects an outgrown youthful enthusiasm for the deistic principles that he describes in an earlier passage of the *Autobiography*,[4] his subsequent account of his failure to reach his goal bespeaks an understanding of human nature in relation to the Divine that owes much more to the theology of Calvin and the Puritans.

The first few generations of American Puritans described the pattern of conversion with remarkable consistency. Though intense flurries of dissent sometimes erupted into major controversy (as in the Antinomian dispute or in the Mather/Stoddard conflict over criteria for admission to communion), the orthodox position on conversion remained relatively stable up until the period of the Great Awakening, when it was torn asunder by attacks of religious liberals advocating freedom of the will on one side, and by Jonathan Edwards' conservative defense (which denied the necessity of a rigid sequence of preparatory stages prior to effectual conversion) on the other. Puritan ministers prior to Edwards had, however, largely insisted on the need for proper preparation of the soul, before a saving faith could be attained, in the form of a series of persuasive works wrought in the heart of the convert by the action of the Holy Spirit.[5] One of the first Americans to describe this process in detail was Thomas Shepard, who in *The Sound Believer* describes it as consisting of a progression from conviction (sight of sin) to compunction (sense of sin) to humiliation (a sense of one's own incapacity to free oneself from sin) to a saving faith in Christ's redemptive power.[6] And even Edwards himself would retain similar concepts as evidence that conversion had occurred, though rejecting them as required preliminary steps.[7]

The net effect of this sequence was to lead the convert to a compelling realization of God's infinite goodness and power through a gradual revelation of his own complete deficiency. At each step, the penitent's knowledge of the binding power of his affinity for sinful ways increased, until he was forced to recognize his utter inability to do good of his own will, and to rely completely on the sufficiency of divine mercy to work redemption in him. Only when he had been brought to this point of abject dependency was he considered adequately prepared for the infusion of divine grace in the form of saving faith. Conviction, as the first step of the process, represented the simple recognition of one's sinfulness and was requisite to the second step, compunction, which Shepard describes as follows:

> Compunction is nothing else but a pricking of the heart, or the
> wounding of the soul with such fear and sorrow for sin as severs the

soul from sin, and from going on toward its eternal misery; so that it consists in three things:—

1. Fear. 2. Sorrow. 3. Separation from sin. [*SB*, p. 146]

In the third stage, humiliation, the subject found that his own best efforts to free himself from sin were unavailing, so that his soul was finally cut off "from all high conceits and self-confidence of that good which is in him, or which he seeks might be in him." (*SB*, p. 175). With this awareness, the soul was prepared to rely exclusively on Christ, and out of that reliance would grow saving faith.

Thus, for the Puritans, salvation was made to depend quite directly upon the full realization of all the negative implications of Original Sin as they related to one's personal condition. Only through an immediate noetic knowledge of mankind's depravity could an understanding of divine perfection be approached. That perfection, furthermore, remained the exclusive property of divinity: the converted saint, no less than the aspiring penitent, could not claim any goodness as his own, and struggled to control his sinful human nature until he was rewarded, after physical death, with the spiritual bliss of eternal heavenly life. The operative assumption, throughout the conversion process, was that sinful habits must be recognized and, with the aid of the Spirit, broken, before they could be replaced with more gracious dispositions. Shepard puts it thus:

> If there have been abundance of sweet affections and sweet refreshings, thereby rising up within the soul, without the death, and killing, and removal of the contrary lusts and sins; it is certain that this soul was never truly filled nor satisfied with the Spirit of God's grace; for as it is with vessels, while they are filled with lime or chaff, they can not be filled with wheat or with water, so while the heart is filled with some noisome distempers, it can not be filled or satisfied with the Lord.[8]

Benjamin Franklin arrives at a similar conclusion even as he introduces his "Project," though his aim of "moral Perfection" is clearly not precisely analogous to the Puritan objective of sanctity. Nevertheless, the first paragraph he devotes to this subject suggests his probable familiarity with the standard Puritan conversion pattern through the attitudes it describes, through its methodical attention to the displacement of bad habits, and even, to a limited extent, through its terminology. He writes:

> It was about this time that I conceiv'd the bold and arduous Project of arriving at moral Perfection. I wish'd to live without committing any Fault at any time; I would conquer all that either Natural Inclination, Custom, or Company might lead me into. As I knew, or thought I knew, what was right and wrong, I did not see why I

might not *always* do the one and avoid the other. But I soon found I had undertaken a Task of more Difficulty than I had imagined. While my *attention was taken up* in guarding against one Fault, I was often surpriz'd by another. Habit took the Advantage of Inattention. Inclination was sometimes too strong for Reason. I concluded at length, that the mere speculative Conviction that it was our Interest to be completely virtuous, was not sufficient to prevent our Slipping, and that the contrary Habits must be broken and good ones acquired and established, before we can have any Dependance on a steady uniform Rectitude of Conduct. [*Autobiography*, p. 148]

Implicitly recognizing his present state of moral imperfection, Franklin's persona resolves to reform by a simple act of will in which he declares his intention to "conquer" his faults. His progress thus far roughly corresponds to that of the Puritan convert through the stages of conviction and compunction, although neither his diction nor his tone provides much indication of either the fear or the sorrow that Shepard associated with the desire to separate oneself from sin. Like Shepard's convert, however, the persona quickly discovers that the reformation process falters despite his own best efforts. "Habit" and "Inclination," both of which Franklin seems to associate with the subconscious will, prove too strong for Reason, confirming the distrust of the intellectual faculty that Franklin has already expressed in explaining his abandonment of his vegetarian diet: "So convenient a thing it is to be a *reasonable Creature*, since it enables one to find or make a Reason for everything one has a mind to do" (p. 88). Shepard would have said that such a man's compunction was not yet completely accomplished, since this work specifically involved a reformation of the will, while conviction affected only the understanding.[9] Franklin retains, in other words, the important Puritan distinction between the regenerative roles of the understanding and the will. One must understand the need to reform before reformation can be possible, but that understanding alone, without a corresponding alteration in one's willful disposition, does not constitute reform.

A similar distinction is reflected in Franklin's use of the term "speculative Conviction," which is itself reminiscent of Shepard's designation for the first stage of preparation. In defining the conviction stage, Shepard elaborates at some length upon an important difference between "rational" and "spiritual" conviction. Though conviction as a whole is associated with the understanding, in Shepard's explanation "rational conviction" develops into something of a pejorative term, designed to indicate a certain lack of firmness and commitment due to shallowness of understanding and perception:

There is a real light in spiritual conviction. Rational conviction
makes things appear notionally; but spiritual conviction, really. The
Spirit, indeed, useth argumentation in conviction; but it goeth
further, and causeth the soul not only to see sin and death
discursively, but also intuitively and really.   [*SB*, p. 127]

Franklin uses "speculative Conviction" to indicate a similar shallowness
and lack of commitment, although his conviction is not of the reality or
immediacy of sin in any theological sense, but rather, of the pragmatic
principle "that it [is] our Interest to be compleatly virtuous." In this case,
the Puritan terminology takes on new denotative meaning, though the
connotation remains largely the same.

    A somewhat different transformation involving both connotative
and denotative differences from the Puritan model occurs in Franklin's
use of the term "humility." Humiliation was the most difficult and des-
perate of the Puritan preparatory stages, and Shepard directed some of
his most vivid prose to the task of evoking a compelling sense of the
penitent's distress at discovering his helplessness:

Hence it comes to pass that the soul, seeing itself to labor only in
the fire and smoke, and to be still as miserable and sinful as ever
before, hereupon it is quite tired out, and sits down weary, not only
of sin, but of its work; and now cries out, I see now what a vile
and undone wretch I am; I can do nothing for God or for myself;
only I can sin and destroy myself; all that I am is vile, and all that
I do is vile: I now see that I am indeed poor, and blind, and
miserable, and naked.   [*SB*, p. 181]

    Like Shepard's convert, Franklin finds that his efforts to control his
behavior fall far short of perfection, even after his conscientious attention
to the cultivation of good habits. Like the customer of his neighbor the
blacksmith, he is forced to conclude that "a speckled Ax is best" (p. 156).
And while this conclusion is qualified by the utilitarian observations "that
a perfect character might be attended with the Inconvenience of being
envied and hated; and that a benevolent man should allow a few Faults
in himself, to keep his Friends in Countenance," it is worth pointing out
that this qualification is itself suggested by a backsliding tendency to
rationalize that Franklin does not permit to pass un-noted: "For something that pretended to be Reason was every now and then suggesting to
me, that such extream Nicety . . . might be a kind of Foppery in Morals."
His distrust of reason remains consistent as Franklin discovers a frustration similar to that of the Puritan's humiliation before he introduces his
own term, "humility." In Franklin's account, however, Shepard's tone of
desperation and self-loathing is replaced by a much milder quality of
bemused, indulgently ironic humor.

Franklin never applies the term "humiliation" to the frustration of his persona's efforts, very probably because its connotation of abasement is incompatible with just this quality of gentle irony. Humiliation is a degrading process to which an individual is subjected. "Humility," however, whatever one may mean by it, is a virtue which an individual may or may not possess. The latter term does not subjugate the individual, and is thus more appropriate to Franklin's purpose of demonstrating the utility of this particular virtue *to* the individual.

Humility proves useful indeed, for in the "extensive meaning" that Franklin attributes to this word is included not only the "Role to forbear all direct Contradiction to the Sentiments of others, and all positive assertion of my own," and the "modest way in which I proposed my opinions" (p. 159), but also the narrative stance that he has chosen to adopt for his continuation of the *Autobiography* beyond the point to which he had brought it at the end of the letter to his son in Part One. The "appearance" of this virtue, even in the absence of its actual possession, is of utilitarian value in that it procures both "readier Reception and less Contradiction" in Franklin's airings of his own proposals, contributing significantly to the worldly success and influence that he cites as evidence of its efficacy. It is no doubt in keeping with these pronouncements that Franklin does not foist the materials of Parts Two and Three upon the reader, but rather tenders them in response to two substantial (and flattering) introductory letters (pp. 133–40) in which they are specifically solicited.

Despite these important distinctions between Franklin's brand of humility and the Puritan concept of humiliation, each occupies a position of key importance at the apex of the reformation process. For Shepard, humiliation is the final stage of preparation, and leads directly into saving faith. For Franklin, humility is apparently the ultimate virtue. It appears last on his list of virtues, and he chooses to end Part Two by defining and discussing it at length. It is (ironically) a virtue which escapes the initial attention of the persona and is suggested to him by a friend (pp. 158–59), but is nonetheless a virtue which, even to the limited extent that the persona is able to practice it, becomes one of his most useful aids in achieving worldly success. Neither the successful Puritan convert nor Franklin's persona is ultimately defeated by the frustrating failure to attain perfection. Though the convert could expect neither to achieve perfect sanctity in earthly life nor to be rewarded specifically because of his efforts to do so, still Shepard and other divines allowed that growth in grace was possible and that the sound believer would continue to increase in degree of holiness, however short of the ideal he might finally fall. The infinite nature of the goal set no limits on the potential amount of finite progress toward it. In much the same way, Franklin's goal of moral perfection proves elusive, but he takes a similar kind of comfort in the improvement that he does see, for all its finite shortcomings: "But on the whole, tho' I never arrived at the Perfection I had been so ambitious of attaining, yet I was by the Endeavor a better and a happier man than I otherwise should have been" (p. 156). His comforts are, however, extended to include specific earthly benefits seldom stressed by Puritan preachers.

As did the Puritans before him, Franklin sees pride as the opposite of humility, and in seriously discussing the possibility of acquiring genuine humility as he closes Part Two, he depicts the struggle to subdue pride in terms that any orthodox Puritan could have applauded:

> In reality there is perhaps no one of our natural Passions so hard to subdue as *Pride*. Disguise it, struggle with it, beat it down, stifle it, mortify it as much as one pleases, it is still alive, and will every now and then peep out and show itself. You will see it perhaps often in this History. For even if I could conceive that I had compleatly overcome it, I should probably by [be] proud of my Humility.   [p. 160]

Jonathan Edwards, in fact, describes a similar difficulty in his *Personal Narrative*. "I have greatly longed of late, for a broken heart, and to lie low before God; and when I ask for humility, I cannot bear the thoughts of being no more humble than other Christians,"[10] Edwards laments, and in his next paragraph goes on to recognize the danger of excessive pride in righteousness:

> I have a much greater sense of my universal, exceeding dependence on God's grace and strength, and mere good pleasure, of late, than I used formerly to have; and have experienced more of an abhorrence of my own righteousness. . . . And yet I am greatly afflicted with a proud and self-righteous spirit, much more sensibly than I used to be formerly. I see that serpent rising and putting forth its head continually, every where, all around me.

Franklin's attempts to demonstrate the worldly utility of virtue clearly do represent a substantial shift of emphasis from the Puritan objective of an otherworldly holiness. They reflect just as clearly, however, a view of human nature that is surprisingly consistent with the Puritans' Calvinistic stress upon the opposition between imperfect man as tarnished by Original Sin, and the ultimate perfection of divinity. Franklin's early deistic leanings, and not the principles of his "Presbyterian" upbringing, are confuted by the facts of his actual experience with human nature, both that of others and his own. After he became a deist, Franklin writes, his arguments "perverted" some others, with the ironic result that his two most stalwart converts "afterwards wronged me greatly without the least Compunction" (p. 114). Equally troubled by his treatment at the hands of Governor Keith (another deist) and by his own treatment of Vernon and Miss Read, Franklin becomes increasingly aware of his own deficiencies, as we have seen, in the course of his efforts to reform. Perhaps his subtlest and most telling touch of irony comes with his poker-faced observation that these efforts, which gradually diminish to the point of nonexistence, are eventually overcome by the press of those very utilitarian affairs that his list of virtues is theoretically designed to help him cope with: "After a while I went thro' one Course only in a Year, and afterwards only one in several Years, till at length I omitted them entirely, being employ'd in Voyages and Business abroad with a Multiplicity of Affairs, that interfered, but I always carried my little Book with me" (p. 155).

These efforts, of course, are not without substantial value, as Franklin takes great pains to point out, but they, no less than the struggles of the Puritan convert, indicate a fundamental weakness of the will and an essentially selfish commitment to one's own interest that can never be completely overcome, and that can be brought under limited control only with the greatest difficulty. The most important difference between Franklin and his Puritan forebears is thus not so much in their views of human nature as in their reactions to those views. Moral perfection and true holiness are equally beyond the capability of mankind, at least during earthly life, but unlike the Puritans, it is only earthly life with which Franklin concerns himself. If man, Franklin seems to conclude, is governed primarily by self-interest despite his nobler aspirations, then earthly happiness must depend on this unfortunate aspect of man's nature, and virtue can be rendered palatable to worldly tastes only insofar as it is related to self-interest. Hence Franklin's stress on the utility of virtue.

It is precisely because of this stress that D. H. Lawrence has accused Franklin of the worst sort of crassly pragmatic materialism.[11] To make such an accusation, however, is to miss the more sensitive implications of the rueful irony with which Franklin underscores his all-too-human weaknesses. In the best of all possible worlds, or in the Puritan heaven, moral perfection and true humility might be attainable, and man's conduct might be governed by some higher principle than self-interest. But Franklin's experience reveals neither this sort of world nor the possibility of changing the world that he does see in any fundamental way. Man is an imperfect creature, and he must learn to live with his imperfections even as he struggles to improve. Franklin's project and the effort required of the candidate for Puritan sainthood are closely analogous in just this respect. They differ in terms of Franklin's reluctant willingness to indulge the undesirable but inescapable attachment to self-interest for purposes of improving life within an admittedly inferior world, where Puritans condemned both that attachment and that world. Franklin's accommodation of virtue to self-interest, which no Puritan would have allowed, can nonetheless be seen as rooted in the Puritan concept of selfish pride as the dominant quality of the natural man. His *Autobiography* provides a particularly instructive example of values in transformation, revealing even closer connections between his Puritan background and his pragmatism than have hitherto been recognized.

NOTES

1. See "Introduction," *The Autobiography of Benjamin Franklin*, ed. Leonard W. Labaree et al. (New Haven and London: Yale University Press, 1964), pp. 17–19; David Levin, "The Autobiography of Benjamin Franklin: The Puritan Experimenter in Life and Art," *Yale Review*, 53 (1964), 261–62; and J. A. Leo Lemay, "Franklin and the *Autobiography*: An Essay on Recent Scholarship," *Eighteenth-Century Studies*, I (1967–68), 202–3. All citations of the *Autobiography* refer to the Yale edition.

2. Larzer Ziff, "Introduction to Benjamin Franklin's Selected Writings," *Benjamin Franklin's Autobiography and Selected Writings* (San Francisco: Rinehart Press, 1969), p. xviii.

3. *Autobiography*, p. 148.

4. See Franklin's misidentified citation of Pope, p. 114:

> Whatever is, is right.
> Tho' purblind Man,
> Sees but a Part of the Chain, the nearest Link
> His eyes not carrying to the equal Beam,
> That poizes all, above.

5. See Norman Pettit, *The Heart Prepared: Grace and Conversion in Puritan Spiritual Life* (New Haven and London: Yale University Press, 1966), pp. 86–114 and 210.

6. In *The Works of Thomas Shepard*, ed. John Albro (1853; rpt. New York: AMS Press, 1967), I, 111–284. Hereafter cited as *SB*.

7. See *A Treatise Concerning Religious Affections*, in *The Works of Jonathan Edwards*, ed. John E. Smith (New Haven and London: Yale University Press, 1959), II, 291 ("conviction"), 311 ("humiliation"), 341 ("conversion"— as Edwards defines it, a term similar in meaning to Shepard's "compunction").

8. *The Parable of the Ten Virgins Opened and Applied*, in *The Works of Thomas Shepard*, II, 481.

9. "Compunction . . . is different from conviction of sin: the latter is the work of the understanding, . . . the other is in the affections and the will." (*SB*, p. 136).

10. *Jonathan Edwards: Representative Selections*, ed. Clarence H. Faust and Thomas H. Johnson (New York: Hill and Wang, 1962), p. 70.

11. See "Benjamin Franklin," *Studies in Classic American Literature* (1923; rpt. New York: Viking, 1964), pp. 9–21.

Cameron C. Nickels   ✿ Franklin's

Poor Richard's Almanacs:
"The Humblest of his Labors"

In Nathaniel Hawthorne's *Biographical Stories for Children* (1842) a child asks his father the reason for the fame of Benjamin Franklin. Not his scientific discoveries nor his political achievements, replies the father; Poor Richard and his maxims are the source of his fame, and the father appropriately concludes with a moral of his own for the child: "Thus it was the humblest of his labors that has done the most for his fame." The boy, however, complains that the maxims have too much to do with getting and saving money. In speaking of Poor Richard and his maxims, the characters in the story undoubtedly refer to Poor Richard's preface to the almanac of 1758, that catalogue of practical wisdom often reprinted as "The Way to Wealth" or "Father Abraham's Speech," which has been Franklin's best-known work for more than two centuries. The preface was popular from the beginning, with one hundred forty-five reprintings in the eighteenth century and countless hundreds through the nineteenth and twentieth centuries. Only recently has the *Autobiography* perhaps replaced "The Way to Wealth" in popular esteem and interest.

From the beginning too, Franklin was identified not merely as the creator of Poor Richard but as Poor Richard himself and the embodiment of the utilitarian philosophy of the famous preface. This confusion of creator and persona seems almost inevitable, considering that the principles the persona embodies and urges so didactically have been identified as a typically American philosophy. Franklin, as Poor Richard, has thus become an early example of an archetypal American character, and, in the words of Charles Sanford, "both a conspicuous target for abuse by critics of American society and a rallying point for defenders of the American 'way of life.' "[1]

Preoccupied with the virtues and vices of American life, however, critics and defenders alike have persistently ignored Franklin's conscious artfulness in method and form in writing the twenty-six almanacs, his most ambitious literary achievement. (As Poor Richard says, "Bad Commentators spoil the best of books.") Franklin's achievement cannot be fully appreciated if we isolate the long series of quotations by Father Abraham from the frame narrative of the 1758 preface and if we isolate the whole preface from the other almanacs that Franklin wrote. As one who enjoyed creating personae and who wrote skillfully in the literary tradition of such great eighteenth-century English prose writers as Swift and Addison, Franklin clearly separated himself from the character he created, Poor Richard Saunders. Artfully conceived and rendered, Poor Richard is a complex, round character that changes over twenty-six years from a rather indolent but affable stargazer to a pompously didactic almanac maker who likes to see himself as an eminent author. Poor Richard should therefore be seen most fundamentally as an "ironic persona," as Irvin Ehrenpreis uses the term, a disguise that must be penetrated if the reader is ultimately to understand that the writer is not in earnest about the views expressed by the persona, but in fact satirizes those views.[2] The preface of 1758 represents the thematic and chronological culmination of Franklin's long literary effort and his brilliantly satiric judgment of all that Poor Richard had become. By creating this kind of dynamic character, by developing him in book after book, and by delineating the character in the contents of the almanacs as well as in the prefaces, Franklin expanded the ostensibly limited artistic possibilities of the almanac genre and raised it to the level of belles lettres.[3]

The distinction between writer and persona is most obvious in the early almanacs, those written in the 1730s. Franklin not only put his own name as printer on the front of the almanacs, but also developed a fictitious relationship between Poor Richard and "the printer" in the prefaces to the almanacs themselves. Franklin established this relationship from the beginning, with Poor Richard's reference in 1733 to the printer's offer of "some considerable share of the Profits" should Richard give in to the demands of his wife, Bridget, to turn his stargazing to profitable use in an almanac.[4] Poor Richard comments more fully upon this relationship in 1739. In six years his almanac has become popular, he admits, although he claims that he has not been enriched, because under the original agreement the printer "runs away with the greatest Part of the Profit." But the philomath does not regret this, for as he says, the printer "is a Man I have a great Regard for, and I wish his Profit ten times greater than it is." Franklin was aware that his readers knew that the printer and the creator of Poor Richard were the same person, and they would appreciate the humorous import of Richard's good will.

Franklin gave full play to his readers' awareness and directly confronted the literary implications of the writer-persona dichotomy by having Richard passionately insist upon an identity separate from that of the printer. The whole of the 1736 preface is given to this issue. Certain ill-wishers, Poor Richard writes, have reported that "I my self was never alive. They say in short, *That there is no such a Man as I am. . . .* This is not civil Treatment, to endeavour to deprive me of my very Being, and reduce me to a Nonentity in the Opinion of the publick." People attribute his yearly productions to the printer, but according to Richard, the printer "is as unwilling to father my Offspring, as I am to lose the Credit of it." In quasi-legal form he declares publicly and seriously, *"That what I have written heretofore, and do now write, neither was nor is written by any other Man or Men, Person or Persons, whatsoever.* Those who are not satisfied with this, must needs be very unreasonable," he concludes.

Franklin further develops this artifice the following year (1737), when Richard writes that if his weather predictions prove inaccurate, it is the fault of the printer, "since in spight of all I can say, People will give him great part of the Credit of making my Almanacks, 'tis but reasonable he should take some of the share of the Blame." In a sense, Franklin adroitly turned upon his own persona the Swiftian trick he had played upon Titan Leeds. In 1733, Poor Richard had regretfully predicted the death of Leeds, a brother philomath, who was, in fact, Franklin's most formidable competitor almanac maker. In subsequent years, Richard indignantly treated Leeds's assertions that he still lived as a cruel joke perpetrated by others. Just as there is no humorous incongruity unless we recognize that Poor Richard wishes Titan Leeds well and Franklin does not, so there is no humor unless we recognize the distinction between Poor Richard and his creator, who also prints the almanacs. Thus was Franklin able to strengthen the identity of the persona, give it breadth, and contribute to the literary potential of the almanac form.

Awareness of the distinction between author and persona is essential too if we are to recognize Franklin's satire of astrological prognostication, satire that appears intermittently but persistently throughout the almanacs. Again, the Leeds hoax served this end in large part. In 1735, Richard argues that it was "requisite and necessary" that Leeds should die punctually at the time that had been predicted "for the honor of Astrology, an Art professed both by him and his Father before him." In Poor Richard's eyes, Leeds did die, proving the worth of the art; to Franklin and the reader, the fact that Leeds continued to live—and argued

vehemently that he did—undercut the efficacy of astrological prognostication. A stargazer turned almanac maker, Poor Richard, the ironic persona,
believes in the philomathic science that was the *raison d'être* of the traditional almanac. A purer scientist, Benjamin Franklin does not share
Richard's faith in a methodology that had long been rejected by men of
learning.

Poor Richard himself admits that astrology has fallen from the
high esteem it once enjoyed, but he argues for its validity as stoutly as he
does for his own identity. Often, however, his arguments are as patently
absurd as his predictions. In 1753 he writes that he is pleased that his
carefully calculated weather predictions seem to satisfy his readers. "I
could almost venture to say, there's not a single One of them, promising
Snow, Rain, Hail, Heat, Frost, Fogs, Wind, or *Thunder,* but what comes
to pass *punctually* and *precisely* on the very Day, in some Place or other
on this little *diminutive* Globe of ours." In 1737 he admits that almanac
makers do sometimes make small mistakes, but they always get the day of
the month correctly. For better accuracy in weather predictions, he modestly asks for "the favourable allowance of *a day or two before* and *a day
or two after* the precise Day against which the Weather is set." Such
earnest arguments, of course, unconsciously substantiate the most fundamental objections to astrological weather predictions and, like his absurd
predictions, clearly separate Richard Saunders from Benjamin Franklin.

Although Franklin satirized prognostication in a number of almanacs, his most concerted attack appeared in 1739. In response to ignorant
men who wonder how astrologers foretell the weather so exactly, Richard
admits that it is "as easy as pissing abed," a conclusion that he supports
with a pseudoscientific, meticulously detailed—and therefore comic—
description of his methods. The almanac ends with "A True Prognostication for 1739," an adaptation of Rabelais' *Pantagruelian Prognostications*
and a catalogue of commonplace truths seriously predicted—that the
blind will see little, the deaf will hear hardly at all, and old age will be
incurable because of the years past, for example. Franklin points up the
satire of Richard's faith in his science with the philomath's belligerent
injunction against those who might find fault with his predictions:

> Take Notice by the by, that having been at a great deal of pains
> in the Calculation, if you don't believe every Syllable, Jot and Tittle
> of it, you do me a great deal of wrong; for which either here or
> elsewhere, you may chance to be claw'd off with a Vengeance. A
> good Cowskin, Crabtree or Bulls pizzle may be plentifully bestow'd
> on your outward Man. You may snuff up your Noses as much as you
> please, 'tis all one for that.

Franklin's most immediate literary model for his satire was surely

Swift's Issac Bickerstaff's *Predictions for the Year 1708*, but satiric attacks
upon almanac makers and parodies of their prognostications had been
popular for more than a century before Franklin or Swift.[5] In fact, Franklin's methods are common to those in the earlier mock almanacs—predictions of things obviously true and of events impossible to verify,
predictions couched in astrological jargon, pugnacious defenses of the
science, and adaptations of Rabelais. For Franklin, however, the satire
not only exposed a foolish faith but served the end of literature as well
by giving further dimension to the characterization of his fictitious philomath. This dimension is nowhere more apparent than in Richard's willful
assumption that his printed predictions do not describe the weather but
rather control it. In writing of the eclipses for 1738, he asks the readers to
excuse him for including no eclipses of the moon for the year. "The Truth
is, I do not find they do you any Good," he says. "When there is one you
are apt in observing it to expose yourselves too much and too long to the
Night Air, whereby great Numbers of you catch Cold. Which was the
Case last Year, to my very great Concern. However, if you will promise
me to take more Care of your selves, you shall have a fine one to stare at,
the Year after next." Franklin thus takes the fact that there were no
eclipses of the moon in 1738 and puts it to literary use to characterize
Poor Richard as the astrologer gone mad, who blithely reverses his true
function of observing heavenly phenomena and assumes that he can control them for what he considers to be the safety and welfare of his reading
public.

Franklin's interest and skill in fully developing the literary potential of the almanac form can be seen as well in his use of the literary
contents of the almanacs—the epigrams, aphorisms, and poetry—to give
further dimension to the character of Poor Richard.[6] Almost none of the
contents were original with Franklin, but he often chose and modified
them to mirror the character of Richard that was drawn in the prefaces
and to reflect Richard's sense of his role as an almanac maker. Franklin
filled the early almanacs, for example, with material that his readers could
easily relate to Richard's stormy marital life with Bridget, who appears
as another character in the almanacs. As Richard writes in the first
preface (1733), he is excessive poor and his wife is excessive proud, and
she cannot bear to sit and spin in her "shift of tow" while he does nothing
but gaze at stars. In fact, she threatens to burn his instruments unless he
makes some profitable use of them for his family. Scattered through the
contents of the almanac are verses about talkative, vain, proud, willful,
as well as properly obedient wives, and epigrams urging drastic action
on the part of husbands: "Ne'er take a wife till thou hast a house (and
a fire) to put her in," and "Love well, whip well." Such sentiments typify
much of the contents of the almanacs from 1733 to 1740.

Franklin's primary sources for the contents of these early almanacs readily provided the kinds of materials he needed for the delineation of Poor Richard. *A Collection of Epigrams* (1735–37) and *Wit's Recreation* (1640), for example, featured dozens of poems that commented with cynical humor on marriage, harried husbands, and difficult wives. Franklin's literary purposes were conveniently served by the fact that a character named "Dick" often appeared in these poems, as in the following, from *A Collection of Epigrams,* which Franklin used in the 1740 almanac:

> My sickly Spouse, with many a Sigh
> Once told me,—Dicky I shall die:
> I griev'd, but recollected strait,
> 'Twas bootless to contend with Fate:
> So Resignation to Heav'ns Will
> Prepar'd me for succeeding Ill;
> 'Twas well it did; for on my life,
> 'Twas Heav'n's Will to spare my Wife.

From the same source, Franklin found an example that nicely suited his characterization of an almanac maker who felt bedeviled by his wife:

> Women are Books, and Men the Readers be,
> Who sometimes in those Books Erratas see;
> Yet oft the Reader's raptur'd with each Line,
> Fair Print and Paper fraught with Sense divine;
> Tho' some neglectful seldom care to read,
> And faithful Wives no more than Bibles heed.
>   Are Women Books? says Hodge, then would mine were
>   An *Almanack,* to change her every Year.   [1737]

When material did not directly suit Franklin's purposes, he modified it to give sharper focus to his literary ends. Bruce Granger shows how Franklin condensed twenty-four lines from the "Fancies and Fantasticks" section of *Wit's Recreation* to create an eight-line verse that more clearly reflects the domestic situation of Richard and Bridget Saunders:

> From a cross Neighbour, and a sullen Wife,
> A pointless Needle, and a broken Knife;
> From Suretyship, and from an empty Purse
>
> . . . .
> From each of these, *Good L—d deliver me.*   [1734][7]

Usually, the modification was only minor. Robert Newcomb argues that the epigram for October 1733, beginning "Time was my Spouse and I could not agree, / Striving for superiority" was used to more fully characterize the relationship of Richard and the determined Bridget.[8] The poem differs from the original only in the first two lines: "Mysus and Mopsa hardly could agree, / Striving about superiority." Franklin's changing of "about" to "for" gently reminds the reader of the real struggle for dominance that characterizes the Saunders' household. Franklin's alteration of Swift's "On His Own Deafness" required a change of only one word, but the intent is clear. Swift's general conclusion, "I hardly hear a Woman's Clack" becomes "I hardly hear my Bridget's Clack" (1739).

Franklin's literary inventiveness required his readers to consider his almanac as an entertaining narrative that continued through almanacs of several years. The poem for December 1733, a husband's complaint against a lazy, proud wife, is answered in the December poem of 1734, "By Mrs. Bridget Saunders . . . in Answer to the December Verses of last Year," a poem that complains of a drinking husband who neglects his family responsibilities. Bridget's indignation reaches its height in the preface of 1738, which she writes for herself to protest the kinds of criticisms that had appeared in earlier almanacs. "What a peascods! cannot I have a little Fault or two, but all the Country must see it in print!" she complains. "They have already been told, at one time that I am proud, another time that I am loud, and that I have got a new Petticoat, and abundance of such kind of stuff." Perhaps specifically recalling the couplet from 1733 that reads, "Many estates are spent in the getting, / Since women for tea forsook spinning and knitting," she complains that "all the World must know, that Poor Dick's Wife has lately taken a fancy to drink a little Tea now and then. A mighty matter, truly, to make a Song of!" It is true, she admits, that she did have a little tea last year, but it was a present from the printer that she could not bear to throw away. Like Franklin's selection of material and the exchange of verses in 1733 and 1734, Bridget's references here to previous almanacs indicate Franklin's intention to give the prefaces and the contents a thematic, literary unity.

The predominantly light, humorous contents give still further embodiment to the characterization of Poor Richard by accurately reflecting his sense of his role as an almanac maker. That is, although he is a serious astrologer, he does not take seriously his other responsibilities as a maker of almanacs, such as providing uplifting wisdom and advice. True, there are occasionally in the early years serious sentiments that reappear in Father Abraham's speech in 1758, but epigrams in the spirit of "Neither a Fortress nor a Maidenhead will hold out long after they begin to parley" are more characteristic of the early contents than "Sloth makes all Things difficult," both of which appear in 1734. In 1733 Poor Richard playfully adds his own name to a list of ruling monarchs; in 1736 he offers a series of "Enigmatical Prophecies," which are in fact only riddles and which he must apologize for the next year. His primary reason for publishing an almanac, he admits in 1733, is to satisfy Bridget's demands for material comfort, not to serve the public good, and with the success of his work in subsequent years he repeatedly confesses that whether or not the public has benefited from his efforts, they have benefited him.

The character of Poor Richard and the contents of his almanacs begin to change in the 1740s, however, when he begins to enjoy the material comfort made possible by the success of his almanac. Reviewing that success in the preface of 1742, he writes that he tries to keep his address a secret from his readers, who constantly pester him to calculate nativities, find runaway livestock, and so forth. "These and the like Impertinences I have now neither Taste nor Leisure for," he complains. The contents of the almanac offer various points of view about Richard's situation. The poem for August, "The Busy Man's Picture," for example, seems to reflect his ambivalent attitude toward success:

> Business, thou Plague and Pleasure of my Life,
> Thou charming Mistress, thou vexatious Wife;
> . . . .
> Some Respite, prithee do, yet do not give,
> I cannot with thee, nor without thee live.

The poem for September, appropriately titled "The Reverse," offers an alternate life style:

> Studious of Ease, and fond of humble Things,
> Below the Smiles, below the Frowns of Kings:
> . . . .
> Content to live, content to die unknown,
> Lord of myself, accountable to none.

In 1744 Richard admits that he has been able to live in comfort by the "Benevolent Encouragement" of the public, but compared to the amiable honesty of earlier years, his address to his readers in this regard appears smugly arrogant. "This is the Twelfth Year that I have in this Way labored for the Benefit—of Whom?—of the Public, if you'll be so good natured as to believe 't; if not, e'en take the naked Truth, 't was for the Benefit of my own dear self; not forgetting in the mean time, our gracious Consort and Dutchess the peaceful, quiet, silent Lady Bridget." The former Bridget is figuratively laid to rest with an adaptation of Dryden's suggested epitaph, which appears at the end of the 1744 almanac: "*Epitaph on a Scolding Wife by her Husband.* Here my poor Bridget's Corps doth lie, she is at rest,—and so am I."

As if recognizing the change in his—and Bridget's—characters, Richard begins the verse preface in 1746 with the question, "Who is Poor Richard? People oft enquire." The meaning of Franklin's poetic syntax is difficult to decipher, but the rest of the poem characterizes Richard and

Bridget as leading a retiring, prudent life, albeit one "with Plenty bless'd." As the contents of the later almanacs reveal, there is nothing of the spirited, self-effacing Richard of the 1730s. With Richard and Bridget living in marital as well as material bliss, there are few humorous illustrations of the vicissitudes of marriage. Indeed, sentiments such as "He that has not got a Wife, is not yet a compleat Man" (1744) and "A good Wife and Health, is man's best Wealth" (1746) mirror the now pacific union of Richard and Bridget. Furthermore, the contents generally tend to exemplify the kind of life style and principles attributed to the Saunders in the 1746 preface.

The kinds of changes that begin to appear in the 1740s are confirmed in 1748, with the change of the title of the almanac to *Poor Richard Improved*. The word "improved" most obviously refers to the enlarged format of the almanac from twenty-four to thirty-six pages, but it also describes the shift in the literary contents of the almanacs, from humorous, entertaining subjects to serious, utilitarian ones. Recalling too that the title is not *Poor Richard's Improved Almanac* or *Poor Richard's Almanac Improved*, we should see that the term applies to Poor Richard himself, to the amelioration of his material condition in which he takes so much pride and to his effort to enhance his reputation as a philomath, an effort that dominates his character after 1748 and reaches its peak ten years later.

Given these changes, the continued use of the adjective "poor" takes on significant meanings. In the early years, of course, the word refers to Richard's poverty, but this meaning no longer applies once his lot has been improved. Poor Richard himself notes this incongruity in three of the almanacs, and in 1742 he uses the word "poor" in the sense that becomes his major concern after 1748. His own success he complains, has produced "a *Poor Will*, a *Poor Robin*; and no doubt a *Poor John*, etc. will follow, and we shall all be *in Name*, what some Folks say we are already *in Fact*. A Parcel of *poor Almanack Makers*." Thus concerned with the lowly status popularly attributed to his occupation, Richard strives in the last decade to improve his own reputation. As he writes in 1750, "The Hope of acquiring lasting FAME, is, with many Authors, a most powerful Motive to Writing. . . . We Philomaths [are] as ambitious of Fame as any other Writers whatever." Contrasted to this ambition, however, is Richard's complaint that most readers examine his work only once and then cast it aside like so much waste paper. Richard is no longer humble, and Franklin's continued use of the adjective "poor" ironically underscores Richard's serious ambitions.

The high seriousness of the contents of the later almanacs should therefore be seen as part of Poor Richard's attempt to give his work a higher purpose, which will in turn create a meaningful and lasting art.

Humor has no place in the concerns of the later Richard. In the preface of 1747 he apologizes for inserting a joke or two, and the 1757 almanac contains several injunctions against the impropriety of imprudent jests, raillery, and unbridled wit. Richard's motives in regard to the contents are made clear in the 1747 preface. The "Astronomical Calculations, and other Things usually contain'd in Almanacks," he writes, "have their daily Use indeed while the Year continues, but then become of no Value." Thus he has "constantly interspers'd moral Sentences, prudent Maxims, and wise Sayings" to make his work more valuable to his readers, a description that he repeats in the 1756 preface. Concerned as he is with his own reputation, Poor Richard's sense of duty is narrowly didactic and self-serving, and his manner obsequious. "'Tis a Pleasure to me to be in any way serviceable in communicating useful Hints to the Public," he writes in 1757. The change in Poor Richard's sense of his role as an almanac maker is clear if we contrast these later statements to one from 1733. Then Richard had written that he would not attempt to gain the readers' favor by saying that he writes only for the public good, for "Men are now-a-days too wise to be deceiv'd by Pretences how specious soever." Yet this is exactly the specious pretense that Richard ultimately uses to try to deceive his readers.

The famous preface of 1758 is an artistically and philosophically appropriate conclusion to Franklin's delineation of Poor Richard, for he gives sharp focus to the fundamental features of Poor Richard's "improved" character and renders a final judgment of them. The first-person point-of-view makes it possible for Poor Richard himself to reveal unconsciously the true emptiness of his foolish pretensions, and the device of the frame story first parodies his didactic stance and then exposes the failure of his utilitarian wisdom. Structurally, the preface must be considered as one of Franklin's finest literary achievements.[9]

In the introductory frame, Poor Richard again agonizes about his lack of public esteem, although his best efforts have been directed toward that goal. "I have heard that nothing gives an Author so great Pleasure, as to find his Works respectfully quoted by other learned Authors." This truism provides thematic direction to the whole preface and an ironic contrast to Poor Richard's confessions about the truth of his own experience. "This Pleasure I have seldom enjoyed," a fact all the more surprising to him because he has been, as he says, "without Vanity, an *eminent Author* of Almanacks annually now for a full Quarter of a Century." Even his brother philomaths "have ever been very sparing in their Applauses," an admission that builds to the flat confession that "no other Author has taken the least Notice of me." Only his own exaggerated sense of his importance blinds him to the true significance of these facts. Ignored by learned authors, he is willing to settle for the approbation of the common people, who have quoted him occasionally. To encourage the practice, he admits, "I have *quoted myself* with great gravity."

This revealing confession serves as an ironic climax to the concern for a lasting reputation that appears as the central feature of Poor Richard's character in the last decade. Concentrated as this concern is in the opening paragraphs of the 1758 preface, it provides an appropriate frame for Father Abraham's harangue of some one hundred quotations from Poor Richard's almanacs. It has been often enough observed that the quotations in the speech are impartially taken from all of the almanacs and that their narrowly utilitarian philosophy is not representative of the wisdom in all of the almanacs. Yet the selections do accurately reflect the general direction that Poor Richard's philosophical interests had taken over the years, and more importantly, the speech itself typifies the didactic stance that he had assumed. The piling on of maxims—all on the same topic, most in the same style, and with the tedious repetition of "as Poor Richard says"—is excessive to the point of absurdity and becomes a caricature of the zealous moralist whose overwhelming desire is that he be quoted. Blinded by this obsession, Poor Richard is merely gratified by Father Abraham's memory. "The frequent Mention he made of me must have tired any one else, but my Vanity was wonderfully delighted with it," he observes.

In the concluding frame, after Father Abraham's speech, Franklin exposes the futility of such wisdom done up for easy recall, however strenuously preached, and thus he underscores the ultimate failure of Poor Richard's repeated effort to make his almanac useful and the basis of his own reputation. One crisp sentence describes the effect of Father Abraham's harangue upon the listening crowd, the people in whom Poor Richard had placed his only faith: "The People heard it, and approved the Doctrine, and immediately practiced the contrary, just as if it had been a common Sermon." (The climactic order of the parallel sentence structure and the comparison at the end—another example of Poor Richard's self-importance—seem worthy of Mark Twain.) Given the inexorable direction of Franklin's intentions in the preface, the conclusion can perhaps be anticipated. Poor Richard can quote himself with gravity, but until reminded by Father Abraham, even he had blithely ignored the substance of his proverbial wisdom. "Though I had at first determined to buy Stuff for a new Coat," he writes, "I went away resolved to wear my old One a little longer." The irony of Richard's forgetfulness is heightened still further if we recall the following advice from the 1756 almanac: "When you incline to have new Cloaths, look first well over the old Ones, and see if you cannot shift with them another Year, either by Scouring, Mending, or even Patching if necessary."

In identifying himself in terms that are ultimately revealed as unfulfilled and in urging as useful a philosophy that is ultimately exposed as impractical, Poor Richard in the later almanacs must be seen as an ironic persona, not as Benjamin Franklin. Franklin was no paltry almanac maker, he did not suffer the neurotic crisis of identity of Poor Richard, and his own interests and philosophical commitments were far broader than the moralisms so doggedly urged by the ambitious philomath. It should be recalled as well in this regard that in 1748, the year that Richard Saunders became "improved," Benjamin Franklin gave up bookselling, turned his printing business over to David Hall, and despite what he modestly called "a little present Run of Popularity," rejected an appeal to run for assemblyman in order to have the leisure to enjoy friends and life in general a little more.[10] Forty years later, in adding to his *Autobiography* in 1788, Franklin did see his almanacs in primarily utilitarian terms "as a proper Vehicle for conveying Instruction among the common People, who bought scarcely any other Books."[11] But such an observation, while it is appropriate to the literary purposes of the *Autobiography*, is not an accurate description of the almanacs. (Franklin also misremembered the publication date of his most famous almanac.) Although perhaps useful by themselves, the contents of the almanacs are made a part of a larger, complex prose narrative. If the theme of that narrative seems to prefigure the archetypal American success story, Franklin's rendering of the theme is more closely akin to the stories of Fitzgerald's rich boys than to the stories of Horatio Alger's poor boys.

NOTES

1. Charles L. Sanford, ed., *Benjamin Franklin and the American National Character*, Readings in American Civilization (Boston: D. C. Heath, 1955), p. v.

2. Irvin Ehrenpreis, "Personae," in *Restoration and Eighteenth-Century Studies: Essays in Honor of Alan Dugald McKillop*, ed. Carroll Camden (Chicago: University of Chicago Press, 1963), p. 34.

3. The best considerations of Poor Richard and the almanacs in essentially literary terms are John J. Ross, "The Character of Poor Richard: Its Source and Alteration." *PMLA*, 55 (September 1940), 785–94; Bruce I. Granger, *Benjamin Franklin: An American Man of Letters* (Ithaca, New York: Cornell University Press, 1964), pp. 51–76; J. A. Leo Lemay, "Benjamin Franklin," in *Major Writers of Early American Literature*, ed. Everett Emerson (Madison, Wisconsin: University of Wisconsin Press, 1972), pp. 211–17.

4. All quotations from the almanacs are taken from *The Papers of Benjamin Franklin*, ed. Leonard W. Labaree et al., which is being published by Yale University Press. Subsequent quotations will be identified by year in the text.

5. See Carroll Camden, "Elizabethan Almanacs and Prognostications," *Library*, 4th Ser., 12 (1934), 83–108, 194–207; F. P. Wilson, "Some English Mock-Prognostications," *Library*, 4th Ser., 19 (1939), 6–43.

6. Robert H. Newcomb, "The Sources of Benjamin Franklin's Sayings of Poor Richard," Diss., University of Maryland, 1957, is an exhaustive study of the sources of the contents of the almanacs.

7. Granger, pp. 73–74.

8. Newcomb, pp. 174–75.

9. Edward J. Gallagher, "The Rhetorical Strategy of Franklin's 'Way to Wealth,'" *Eighteenth-Century Studies*, 6 (1973), 475–85, is the most complete analysis of the structure of the preface. See also Lemay, pp. 215–17.

10. Letter to Cadwallader Colden, Sept. 29, 1748, *Papers*, III, 318.

11. *The Autobiography of Benjamin Franklin*, ed. Leonard W. Labaree et al. (New Haven: Yale University Press, 1964), p. 164.

J. A. Leo Lemay · ❧ The Text, Rhetorical

Strategies, and Themes of "The Speech

of Miss Polly Baker"

The version of "The Speech of Miss Polly Baker" generally regarded as the best text is in the London *General Advertiser* of April 15,
1747. Max Hall showed that this was the first printed copy of the Speech
and used it as copy-text in his careful edition.[1] Following Hall, the editors
of *The Papers of Benjamin Franklin* accept it as the best text.[2] The
provenance of the *General Advertiser* text remains a puzzle. How did a
London newspaper that seems to have had no connection with Franklin
become the first paper to print his hoax? The most likely explanation is
that Franklin gave copies of the Speech to a few friends, that other
copies were transcribed from those in circulation, and that, ultimately, a
copy—probably a transcription—came to the attention of the editor-
publisher of the *General Advertiser*.[3] We know that giving copies of
bagatelles was a common eighteenth-century practice and that several
of Franklin's satires circulated extensively in manuscript before their first
publication.[4] Without confirming evidence, this explanation of the source
of the *General Advertiser* text remains a mere hypothesis, albeit most
probable.

Whenever Franklin transcribed a copy of his Speech of Polly Baker,
he probably slightly changed the text, sometimes improving it for stylistic
reasons, and sometimes altering it for a particular audience. I believe that
he made such alterations and that as a result of Franklin's revisions, at
least two authentic texts of Polly Baker are extant. But the aesthetically

better text has generally been ignored. Max Hall (following a lead supplied by Whitfield J. Bell, Jr.) and J. F. S. Smeall, at approximately the same time, both called attention to the significantly different text of "The Speech of Miss Polly Baker" printed in the *Maryland Gazette* of August 11, 1747. In the first part of this essay, I will attempt to prove that this text is stylistically superior to and more dramatic than the *General Advertiser* text, that its references to colonial American institutions and customs are more accurate, and that those passages unique to it are, like the rest of the speech, by Franklin.[5] Since the *Maryland Gazette* text is not widely available, I will reprint it here, with superscript letters keyed to the substantive differences between it and the *General Advertiser* text. A note, evidently by Jonas Green, the editor of the *Maryland Gazette*, prefaces the text:

> The following very famous SPEECH has been published in the *London* and *Gentleman's Magazines* for *April* past, as well as in some other *British* Papers; but was there printed incorrectly, which I suppose was occasioned by the Mutilation it suffer'd, in passing through the Hands of Transcribers before it reach'd the Press in *London*: And happening to have a correct Copy of it by me, I cannot think it amiss to give it my Readers, not doubting it's favourable Reception.

> *The SPEECH of Miss* Polly Baker, *before a Court of Judicature, at* Connecticut[a] *in* New England, *where she was prosecuted the fifth Time for having a Bastard Child; which influenced the Court to dispense with her Punishment, and induced one of her Judges to marry her the next Day.*
>   MAY it please the Honourable Bench to indulge me[b] a few Words: I am a poor unhappy Woman; who have no Money to Fee Lawyers to plead for me, being hard put to it to get a tolerable Living. I shall not trouble your Honours with long Speeches; for I have not the presumption to expect, that you may, by any Means, be prevailed on to deviate in your Sentence from the Law, in my Favour. All I humbly hope is, that your Honours would charitably move the Governor's Goodness on my Behalf, that my Fine may be remitted. This is the Fifth Time, Gentlemen, that I have been dragg'd before your Courts[c] on the same Account; twice I have paid heavy Fines, and twice have been brought to public Punishment, for want of Money to pay those Fines. This may have been agreeable to the Laws; I do[d] not dispute it: But since Laws are sometimes unreasonable in themselves, and therefore repealed; and others bear too hard on the Subject in particular Circumstances;

and therefore there is left a Power somewhere[e] to dispense with the
Execution of them; I take the Liberty to say, that I think this Law,
by which I am punished, is both unreasonable in itself, and
particularly severe with regard to me, who have always lived an
inoffensive Life in the Neighbourhood where I was born, and defy
my Enemies (if I have any) to say I ever wrong'd Man, Woman or
Child. Abstracted from the Law, I cannot conceive (may it please
your Honours) what the Nature of my Offence is. I have brought
Five fine Children into the World, at the Risque of my Life: I have
maintained them well by my own Industry, without burthening the
Township, and could[f] have done it better, if it had not been for the
heavy Charges and Fines I have paid. Can it be a Crime (in the
Nature of Things I mean) to add to the Number of the King's
Subjects, in a new Country that really wants People? I own[g] I should
think it[h] rather a Praise worthy, than a Punishable Action. I have
debauch'd no other Woman's Husband, nor inticed any[i] innocent
Youth: These Things I never was charged with; nor has any one
the least cause of Complaint against me, unless, perhaps the
Minister, or[j] the Justice, because I have had Children without being
Married, by which they have miss'd a Wedding Fee. But, can even[k]
this be a Fault of mine? I appeal to your Honours. You are pleased
to allow I don't want Sense; but I must be stupid[l] to the last Degree,
not to prefer the honourable State of Wedlock, to the Condition I
have lived in. I always was, and still am, willing to enter into it;[m]
I doubt not my Behaving well in it, having all the Industry,
Frugality, Fertility, and Skill in Oeconomy, appertaining to a good
Wife's Character. I defy any Person to say I ever Refused an Offer
of that Sort: On the contrary, I readily Consented to the only
Proposal of Marriage that ever was made me, which was when I
was a Virgin; but too easily confiding in the Person's Sincerity that
made it, I unhappily lost my own Honour, by trusting to his; for
he got me with Child, and then forsook me: That very Person you
all know; he is now become a Magistrate of this County;[n] and I had
hopes he would have appeared this Day on the Bench, and have
endeavoured to moderate the Court in my Favour; then I should
have scorn'd to have mention'd it; but I must[o] Complain of it as
unjust and unequal, that my Betrayer and Undoer, the first Cause
of all my Faults and Miscarriages (if they must be deemed such)
should be advanced to Honour and Power, in the[p] same Government
that punishes my Misfortunes with Stripes and Infamy. I shall[q] be
told, 'tis like, that were there no Act of Assembly in the Case, the
Precepts of Religion are violated by my Transgressions. If mine,
then, is a religious Offence, leave it,[r] Gentlemen, to religious

Punishments. You have already excluded me from[s] all the Comforts
of your Church Communion: Is not that sufficient? You believe I
have offended Heaven, and must suffer eternal Fire: Will not that
be sufficient? What need is there, then, of your additional Fines and
Whippings?[t] I own, I do not think as you do; for, if I thought, what
you call a Sin, was really such, I would[u] not presumptuously commit
it. But how can it be believed, that Heaven is angry at my having
Children, when, to the little done by me towards it, God has been
pleased to add his divine Skill and admirable Workmanship in the
Formation of their Bodies, and crown'd it by furnishing them with
rational and immortal Souls? Forgive me Gentlemen, if I talk a
little extravagantly on these Matters; I am no Divine: But if you,[v]
great Men,[*] must be making Laws, do not turn natural and useful
Actions into Crimes, by your Prohibitions.[w] Reflect a little on the
horrid Consequences of this Law in particular: What Numbers of
procur'd Abortions! and how many distress'd Mothers have been
driven, by the Terror of Punishment and public Shame, to imbrue,
contrary to Nature, their own trembling Hands in the Blood of their
helpless Offspring! Nature would have induc'd them to nurse it up
with a Parent's Fondness. 'Tis the Law therefore, 'tis the Law itself
that is guilty of all these Barbarities and Murders. Repeal it then,
Gentlemen; let it be expung'd for ever from your Books: And on
the other hand, take into your wise Consideration, the great and
growing Number of Batchelors in the Country, many of whom, from
the mean Fear of the Expence[x] of a Family, have never sincerely
and honourably Courted a Woman in their Lives; and by their
Manner of Living, leave unproduced (which[y] I think is little better
than Murder) Hundreds of their Posterity to the Thousandth
Generation. Is not theirs[z] a greater Offence against the Public
Good, than mine? Compel them then, by a[aa] Law, either to Marry,[ab]
or pay double the Fine of Fornication every Year. What must poor
young Women do, whom Custom has[ac] forbid to solicit the Men, and
who cannot force themselves upon Husbands, when the Laws take
no Care to provide them any, and yet severely punish[ad] if they do
their Duty without them?[ae] Yes, Gentlemen, I venture to call it a
Duty; 'tis the Duty of the first and great Command of Nature, and of
Nature's God, *Increase and multiply*: A Duty, from the steady
Performance of which nothing has[af] ever been able to deter me;
but for it's Sake, I have hazarded the Loss of the public Esteem,
and frequently incurr'd[ag] public Disgrace and Punishment; and

[*] *Turning to some Gentlemen of the Assembly, then in Court.*

therefore ought, in my humble Opinion, instead of a Whipping, to have a Statue erected to my Memory.

Substantive differences between the *Maryland Gazette* text (before the half bracket) and the *General Advertiser* text (following the half bracket):

a. Connecticut *in*] *Connecticut* near *Boston* in

b. me a] me in a

c. Courts] Court

d. do not] don't

e. somewhere] somewhat

f. could] would

g. own I] own it, I

h. it rather a Praise worthy, than] it a Praise-worthy, rather than

i. any innocent Youth] any Youth

j. or the Justice] or Justice

k. even] ever

l. stupid] stupified

m. it; I doubt] it and doubt

n. County] Country

o. must Complain] must now Complain

p. the same Government] the Government

q. shall] should

r. it, Gentlemen, to] it to

s. from all the] from the

t. Whippings] Whipping

u. would] could

v. you, great men,* [marginal note follows:] * *Turning to some Gentlemen of the Assembly, then in Court.*] Gentlemen, must

w. Prohibitions. Reflect a little on the horrid Consequences of this Law in particular: What Numbers of procur'd Abortions! and how many distress'd Mothers have been driven, by the Terror of Punishment and public Shame, to imbrue, contrary to Nature, their own trembling Hands in the Blood of their helpless Offspring! Nature would have induc'd them to nurse it up with a Parent's Fondness. 'Tis the Law therefore, 'tis the Law itself that is guilty of all these Barbarities and Murders. Repeal it then, Gentlemen; let it be expung'd for ever from your Books: And on the other hand, take into] Prohibitions. But take into

x. Expence] Expences

y. which I think is] which is

    z. theirs] this
  aa. by a Law] by Law
  ab. Marry, or pay] Marriage or to pay
  ac. has] have
  ad. punish if] punish them if
  ae. them? Yes, Gentlemen, I venture to call it a Duty; 'tis the
      Duty] them; the Duty
  af. has ever been] has been
  ag. and frequently incurr'd] and have frequently endured

The editor of the *Maryland Gazette,* Jonas Green, claims that his text is a "correct Copy" of the Speech, and impugns the text published in the *"British* Papers." Green accounts for the supposedly incorrect printing "by the Mutilation it suffer'd, in passing through the Hands of Transcribers before it reach'd the Press in *London."* Thus Green suspects that the English text was transmitted exactly as we would think it had been, even if we did not have Green's contemporary opinion. In refuting Green's claims to the validity and superiority of the *Maryland Gazette* text, Max Hall and the editors of *The Papers of Benjamin Franklin* suggest that Green may have himself tampered with the Speech and that he was, in this prefatory note, simply puffing himself and his paper. But this reasoning seems far-fetched. It was natural for Green, Dr. Alexander Hamilton, and other Maryland litterateurs to know of Franklin's bagatelle and to have copies of it. That Green himself, who had formerly worked in Philadelphia as a printer and who corresponded with Franklin,[6] was knowledgeable concerning Franklin's hoaxes at this precise period (the summer of 1747) is proved by his reprinting Franklin's anonymous "Verses on the Virginia Capitol Fire" in the *Maryland Gazette,* June 16, 1747. Green wrote Franklin on July 25, 1747, that "The Virginian's Speech made a deal of Laughter here; and was well approved of by some in that Colony." Green knew, of course, that Franklin's travesty of Governor Gooch's speech must have upset and angered Sir William Gooch, but he slyly added "how the Baronet himself lik'd it I have not heard" (P, III, 154). What makes Green's letter especially telling is that Franklin obviously did not want Governor Gooch to know that he wrote the burlesque. For this reason, Franklin published the "Verses" in James Parker's newspaper in New York and did not print it in his *Pennsylvania Gazette.* Less than two months after Green reprinted Franklin's "Verses on the Virginia Capitol Fire," the Maryland printer published his "correct Copy" of The Speech of Polly Baker. Green's printing of Franklin's "Verses on the Virginia Capitol Fire" and his letter to Franklin prove a hypothesis that we would naturally assume: Jonas Green and the Maryland literary circle generally knew the best writings of their friends and neighbors to the north. Nevertheless, despite Green's direct statement in the *Maryland Gazette* and despite the supporting evidence of his knowledge of Franklin's satires, I concede that the external evidence concerning the authenticity of Green's version of The Speech of Polly Baker, while strong, is not conclusive.

The internal evidence, however, is cogent. Let us begin by comparing the shortest and least convincing differences between the two texts of Polly Baker. In some very few ways, the *General Advertiser* (*GA*) text seems better. It is more effective in three details: "f" ("would" rather than "could"), "o" ("must now Complain" rather than "must Complain"), and "u" ("could" rather than "wou'd")—though one might argue that "f" and "u" contain negligible differences. In two other instances, the English text seems more colloquial: "d" ("don't" rather than "do not") and "m" ("it and doubt" rather than "it; I doubt"), though one might counter that the *Maryland Gazette* (*MG*) text of "d" is more emphatic and of "m" is clearer. Nevertheless, I grant that in these five details, the *General Advertiser* text is, on the whole, better. Further, in eight instances, the choice between the two texts seems optional: "l" (I prefer the more distinctive and remarkable "stupified" of the *GA* text; but my students generally prefer, partly because it sounds more natural, the *MG* "stupid"); "q" (*GA* "should" rather than *MG* "shall"—but if one argues that the *GA* "f" and "u" are more effective, one could argue that the *MG* "q" is more effective); "t" (though *MG* "Whippings" is more accurate and better balanced than *GA* "Whipping"); "y" (one could argue either that *GA* "which is" is more concise or that *MG* "which I think is" has a more appealing ethos); "z" (*GA* "this" or *MG* "theirs"); "aa" (*MG* "by a Law" is less concise but more accurate than *GA* "by Law"); "ab" (*GA* "Marriage or to pay" or *MG* "Marry, or pay"); and "ag" (*GA* "and have frequently endured," which has more pathos—or *MG* "and frequently incurr'd," which is more concise).

Against the five examples where the English text might be thought superior (and the eight differences where the choice seems optional), there are twenty instances in which the American text is, I believe, superior. The weakest of these concern better diction in "k" (*GA* "ever" is evidently an error in transcription for the *MG* "even"—this identical error was made in another contemporary transcription of Franklin's handwriting),[7] and "x" (*GA* "Expences" rather than *MG* "Expence"—though this is negligible). In two cases *MG* is more concise: "b" (*GA* adds "in") and "ad" (*GA* adds "them"); and in "h," *MG* ("it rather a Praise worthy than") is clearer and better balanced than *GA* ("it a Praise-worthy, rather than"). So far, the score (five for the *GA* text, eight optional, and five for the *MG* text) is about even, but now we come to the more significant internal evidence.

A chief general difference between the two texts is that the American text more accurately reflects the conditions of American law, government, and culture. Thus "c" (*MG* "Courts" rather than *GA* "Court"), "e" (*MG* "somewhere" rather than *GA* "somewhat"), "j" (otherwise the minister and justice tend to become synonyms), and especially "n" and "v" all indicate that the author was familiar with American culture and with the machinery of American government. Laws were made by the members of Assembly—not by the magistrates ("v"); and the judges who would hear a trial for fornication would not be judges of the "Country" but of the "County" ("n"). (As I shall suggest below, Franklin may have preferred the inaccurate "Country" for the sake of a salacious pun.) These five differences between the two texts all suggest that the *General Advertiser* text was composed for an English audience, an audience which would neither know nor care about the accuracy with which American customs were reflected. The different audiences of the two texts explain the reason for the key change in "a," for the English audience might not know where Connecticut was and would not have any special feelings about it; so it was identified as being "near *Boston*," which the English generally associated with Puritanism, fanaticism, and harsh laws regarding morals.[8] On the other hand, Americans not only knew where Connecticut was, but they also knew the common oral stories about Connecticut's "blue laws,"[9] and Franklin himself used this tradition of American humor.[10] The words in the heading "near Boston" must have been added for an English audience—and if Franklin did not insert them himself, then this throws doubt upon the entire *General Advertiser* text. But I believe that the English text is also authentic, for it seems to me most unlikely that anyone other than the composer of the original Polly Baker would have made these six distinctions in the text to accommodate the different audiences for which these two texts were intended. As for the literary superiority within this category (of changes made with a view to the different audiences), "v," with its greater dramatic effect in the American text, seems intrinsically superior to the English text, but the inaccurate "Country" ("n") in the English text, because of the pun, is more fun.

The *Maryland Gazette* text is more dramatic in three other instances: "p" (*MG* "the same Government" rather than *GA* "the Government"), "r" (wherein *MG* reminds the reader of the dramatic context by inserting the direct address "Gentlemen"), and "ae." Since "ae" (a relatively long addition: "Yes, Gentlemen, I venture to call it a Duty; 'tis the") is part of the peroration, its greater dramatic quality is enhanced by its rhetorical position. Further, "s" (*MG* "from all the" rather than *GA* "from the") and "af" (*MG* "has ever been" rather than *GA* "has been") are both more effective in the American text; and *MG* "i" ("any innocent

Youth" rather than *GA* "any Youth") seems clearly better, in part because it is more believable. Thus, without considering the greatest single difference between the two texts, the *Maryland Gazette* text appears to be aesthetically superior and more accurate.

The major difference, "w," between the two texts is the only one that has been specifically considered by Max Hall and the editors of *The Papers of Benjamin Franklin* in adjudging the authorship of the *MG* text and in considering its merits. Max Hall calls this passage on the murder of bastard infants a "heavy-handed passage" which "does not match the style of the rest of the speech" (p. 121). The editors of *The Papers of Benjamin Franklin* (III, 147) agree that the "style" of this section is unlike Franklin. But Max Hall himself proved (p. 123) that the style was typical of Franklin, for he cited six examples (supplied by the authority on Franklin's style, Verner W. Crane) wherein Franklin used nearly identical diction and syntax. I will endeavor below to show how this passage clashes with the rest of the Speech (and the good reasons why it does), but a consideration of the most important single source of The Speech of Polly Baker (a source echoed in this passage) will confirm my two-edged argument: the American text is superior aesthetically, and Franklin wrote it.

No one has pointed out that the conclusion of The Speech of Polly Baker—in which she proposes that she "ought, in my humble Opinion, instead of a Whipping, to have a Statue erected to my Memory"—alludes to the most famous satire in English literature. The outrageousness of Polly Baker's proposal echoes that of the projector (the impractical visionary idealist) who claims that "whoever could find out a fair, cheap, and easy Method of making these Children sound and useful Members of the Commonwealth, would deserve so well of the Public *as to have his Statue set up* for a Preserver of the Nation"[11] (my italics). The projector, of course, is the fictive mask of Jonathan Swift in *A Modest Proposal for Preventing the Children of Poor People from Being a Burthen to their Parents, or the Country, and for making them Beneficial to the Publick.* Scholars have frequently noted that Jonathan Swift was a dominant influence upon Franklin; and I believe that his stylistic influence was probably more important than that of any other author, excepting the little-known but prolific writer for the *New England Courant,* Nathaniel Gardner. Every very knowing American would have recognized the allusion at the end of the Speech. The allusion places the Speech in the tradition of hoaxes and satires, and tends, by its association of Polly Baker with the inhuman projector of the *Modest Proposal,* to undercut her character.

Another echo of the *Modest Proposal* exists in the Speech.[12] Swift had written of the projector's concern for mothers who murder their children.

> *There* is likewise another great Advantage in my *Scheme,* that it will
> prevent those *voluntary Abortions,* and that *horrid Practice of*
> *Women murdering their Bastard Children*; alas! too frequent among
> us, sacrificing the *poor innocent* Babes, I doubt, more to avoid the
> Expense than the Shame, which would move Tears and Pity in the
> most Savage and inhuman Breast.

Swift's sentiment is echoed in the long passage ("w") containing 97 words
unique to the *Maryland Gazette* text. Whoever added this passage to the
Speech of Polly Baker (or composed it as part of the original) knew that
he was making another allusion to Swift's *Modest Proposal.* It is most
unlikely that an additional allusion to Swift's great satire would have
been written by anyone other than the original author—and to argue that
it was added by Jonas Green, is implicitly to argue that Green had the
literary genius of Franklin. Since the passage on the murder of bastard
infants unique to the *Maryland Gazette* text alludes to a key source used
elsewhere in the Speech, I believe that the passage should, for this
reason alone, be regarded as an authoritative part of the Speech and as
composed by Franklin.

   The passage adds a more serious note of satire to the Speech.
Franklin might want to omit it from a text intended for an English audience for a number of good reasons—especially because he could foresee that
the Speech might be used as an anti-American satire. (New England blue
laws were a common subject of English prejudice and of American spoof-
ing.)[13] And I will argue, in considering the rhetorical strategies and
themes of the Speech, that this passage, as well as the various other
additions of some length, all make the *Maryland Gazette* text a more
complex, interesting and effective satire. But even before taking up these
considerations, I believe that the internal evidence already adduced
makes an overwhelmingly strong case for Franklin's authorship of the
Maryland Gazette text of The Speech of Miss Polly Baker. The cumula-
tive weight of the internal evidence considered thus far and of the external evidence makes Franklin's authorship of the *Maryland Gazette*
version of The Speech of Polly Baker certain.

   In either text, the Speech is rhetorically intricate, but an examination of Franklin's themes and strategies will prove that the *Maryland*
Gazette text is both better unified and more complex. The rhetorical
handbooks studied by every educated person of the eighteenth and preceding centuries commonly contained a section on the proofs, which
consisted of *ethos,* or establishing the speaker's good character and
credibility; *pathos,* or arousing the feelings of the audience; and *logos,*
or using arguments, generally syllogistic reasoning, to make one's point.[14]
Every sentence in the Speech contains at least one rhetorical proof. Let

us first briefly consider the ethical proof. The Speech opens with Polly
Baker establishing her respectful attitude and humble posture: "MAY it
please the Honourable Bench to indulge me a few Words." She has "not
the presumption to expect" that the magistrates will "deviate" from the
law in her behalf. She has never done anyone any injury: I "defy my
Enemies (if I have any) to say I ever wrong'd Man, Woman or Child."
She is hard working and frugal, a husbandless mother who has "maintained" her children "well" by her "own Industry." She has done a public
service by adding "to the Number of the King's Subjects, in a new
Country that really wants People." She would make a good wife and has
"all the Industry, Frugality, Fertility, and Skill in Oeconomy, appertaining to a good Wife's Character." She owes her downfall to her too honest
and trusting nature: "I unhappily lost my own Honour, by trusting to
his." She stoically bears her misfortunes: "I should have scorn'd to have
mention'd it." She is not a presumptuous sinner, but something of a partner with God (!) in the production of children. She modestly apologizes
for her extravagances in talking about religion: "I am no Divine." And
she perseveres in her duty despite overwhelming odds. Her good qualities
(respectful, humble, harmless, industrious, frugal, public-spirited,
motherly, trusting, forebearing, enduring, loving, Christian, and dutiful)
certainly establish Polly Baker's strong ethical position.

Franklin also put the proof of pathos, that is, of appealing to the
sympathies of the audience, to good use. Polly Baker claims that she is "a
poor unhappy Woman" with "no Money to Fee Lawyers to plead for me."
She says that she has been "dragg'd before your Courts" five times, fined
twice, and was twice "brought to public Punishment, for want of Money
to pay those Fines." The law, she argues, is "particularly severe with
regard to me." She risked her life in having children. Moreover, she is a
wronged virgin, the victim of a consciousless magistrate. She has, paradoxically, lost her honor because she is a woman of honor. She is socially
ostracized, excluded "from all the Comforts" of "Church Communion." In
the conclusion, she asks what "poor young Women" must do, when the
laws do not provide them with husbands. She maintains that she has
done her Christian duty, enjoined by the Bible, despite fines and whippings. In addition, many of the ethical arguments also appeal to the
sympathies of the audience, especially Polly's portrayal of herself as a
husbandless mother, striving against overwhelming odds to rear her five
children.

The third and final kind of "inartificial proof" open to a classical
orator was *logos*, or proving the case by reasoning.[15] Franklin was, of
course, a brilliant logical thinker and a believer in the inductive method
of scientific proof. In his scientific writings, he constructed theories and
designed proofs that would test them.[16] As he wrote at the end of his

argument concerning his best-known single hypothesis, the electrical nature of lightning—"Let the experiment be made."[17] At the same time, Franklin delighted in false arguments to undercut a point. He was generally suspicious of syllogistic reasoning;[18] and he often used false logic to suggest that the opposite point of view from that being urged by his obtuse persona was correct.[19] And Polly Baker's arguments are based upon syllogistic reasoning. She uses a double syllogism in the argument: "But since Laws are sometimes unreasonable in themselves, and therefore repealed; and others bear too hard on the Subject in particular Circumstances . . ." The major premise of the first syllogism is "Laws are sometimes unreasonable in themselves and therefore repealed"; the minor premise asserts—but does not prove—that this law is unreasonable in itself; and the conclusion, of course, is that the law should be repealed. (I should point out, that a direct statement of the long-delayed conclusion is found only in the *Maryland Gazette* text, in "w"). The major premise of the other syllogism is Laws sometimes "bear too hard on the Subject in particular circumstances—and therefore their execution may be ameliorated"; the minor premise is This law is "particularly severe with regard to me"; and the implied conclusion (given statement at the end of the speech) is that no punishment should be exacted in her (or, it is implied, in any other) case.

Polly Baker also uses a well-known logical fallacy, a *petitio principii*, that is, assuming one of the premises, in her argument. Her major premise is that any woman of sense would rather be married than single; her minor premise is "You are pleased to allow I don't want Sense"; and the conclusion of course is that she would prefer to be married. But insofar as we know, the magistrates have not said that she doesn't "want sense." (Incidentally, in one jotting in his marginalia, Franklin quarreled with an English author for just this logical failure: "By this word [Dependencies] you assume what is not granted; and all that follows is therefore unfounded"—P, XVII, 387.) Even if the magistrates granted it, the whole point is irrelevant; the argument is, as Franklin well knew, an *ignoratio elenchi*, or a red herring: for this argument obviously changes the subject and dodges the issue.

So too does Polly Baker's argument that she has not committed a religious offense. Besides, if put as a syllogism, the major premise is a *petitio principii*. Major premise: God does not create people and give them souls if he does not approve of their origin; minor premise: her children have souls; conclusion: God approves of her having children. (Note that this same argument could be used to justify rape if children resulted.) This argument is both an example of the *argumentum ad verecundiam* (the appeal to traditional values) and a well-known topic in the invention of arguments, the argument from consequences. So too is Polly Baker's argument for philoprogenitiveness: "Can it be a Crime . . . to add to the Number of the King's Subjects, in a new Country that really wants People?" Although Aristotle admits the argument from consequences as one of the twenty-eight valid topics,[20] the argument is, in this case, obviously a red herring. Polly Baker also turns the argument against the accuser or judges—another (the sixth) of Aristotle's valid topics—thus undercutting their implied moral superiority. But, of course, a crime is not right merely because a judge has committed it.

Franklin's favorite ruse is the most famous and glaring logical fallacy—the *reductio ad absurdam*. When Polly Baker maintains that she cannot conceive what the nature of her offense is, and maintains that she gave birth to her children "at the Risque" of her life, and brought them up "by my own Industry," and proclaims that she thinks it "rather a Praise worthy, than a Punishable Action"—the entire sequence is a *reductio ad absurdam*. The readers know that, for prostitutes, children are an undesired by-product of the profession. Polly thus inverts the normal feeling and carries it to a ridiculous conclusion. A more concise *reductio* is Polly Baker's reducing the only possible "Cause of Complaint against" herself to one made by "the Minister, or the Justice, because I had Children without being Married, by which they have miss'd a Wedding Fee." But this venal sin is not her fault, for she is and always has been willing to marry. Even more obviously absurd is the charge against bachelors: "by their Manner of Living," bachelors "leave unproduced . . . Hundreds of their Posterity to the Thousandth Generation," which is, Polly assures us, "little better than murder." And the masterpiece of drawing out a farfetched argument to its ultimate implication is found in the conclusion of the speech, where Polly argues that she has been religiously following the duty enjoined on her by the Bible, "A Duty, from the steady performance of which, nothing could deter me."

Of course, the whole Speech is an example of false logic, for Polly Baker begs the essential question (did she commit fornication?) and addresses only a possible consequence of fornication (having bastards). The law is not against illegitimate children—but against fornication outside of wedlock; bastards are simply one proof that fornication took place.[21] Nothing said by Polly Baker attempts to reply to the actual law. Thus the entire Speech is a logical irrelevance, an *ignoratio elenchi*. But this is only suitable, for Franklin has deliberately created an ironic, obtuse persona in Polly Baker. And the persona, like the logic, is another aspect of Franklin's rhetorical strategy in the Speech.

Polly Baker is a naif. She does not understand what her crime is. She seems to think that she is in court for having children. The only time she alludes to the actual law is in her digression on bachelors, who should be compelled to marry or to "pay double the Fine of Fornication every year." Baker says that she cannot "conceive" what the nature of her crime is, she combines the quality of a naif with those of an obtuse persona. But it is a particular kind of obtuseness, having overtones of true moral vision. (We recall Franklin's disgust with the human race in his letter of June 7, 1782, to Joseph Priestley: "for without a Blush they assemble in great armies at NoonDay to destroy, and when they have kill'd as many as they can, they exaggerate the Number to augment the fancied Glory; but they creep into Corners, or cover themselves with the Darkness of night, when they mean to beget, as being asham'd of a virtuous Action.")[22] The combination of seeming obtuseness and of true superior morality is typical of the foreign-observer persona. Polly Baker exemplifies the literary usefulness as well as the characteristics of this persona. In bringing to her trial not only a lack of knowledge of the technical laws of New England but also an unbelievably obtuse ignorance of the common mores and standards of behaviour of Western civilization, Polly Baker calls these mores and standards into question. This naive-obtuse-moral point of view is a splendid disguise for the skeptical and relativistic qualities of mind of her creator, Benjamin Franklin, whom Condorcet, at least, believed to be a Pyrrhonist.[23] Significantly, both the letter to Priestley and the essay on American Indians ("Savages, we call them, because their Manners differ from ours, which we think the Perfection of Civility; they think the same of theirs.")[24] echo Montaigne, whose skeptical outlook (Montaigne was considered the epitome of Pyrrhonism in Franklin's favorite early handbook on logic) is more akin to the fundamental, private Franklin than is the deistic optimism that he so frequently and so successfully affected.[25]

Before turning to the themes and the accomplishments of the Speech, we should examine another element in its rhetorical strategy—its use and burlesque of the structure of the classical oration. The heading is the *exordium* to Polly's oration, catching the attention of the reader, making him wonder what a hardened prostitute (a five-time offender) could say in her own defense, and especially arousing his curiosity about what could influence the court to "dispense with her Punishment." And the heading also must cause the reader to wonder, incredulously, what could possibly "induce one of her Judges to marry her the next Day." Of course, the contrast is funny (a judge marrying a prostitute!), as is just the idea of anyone marrying after a single day's courtship. Thus the heading alone tells the reader that the piece is a *jeu d'esprit* (and only a naive reader or one with an *idée fixe* would not recognize that the speech was going to be a spoof). The title further reveals the outcome of this dramatic and possibly apprehensive situation (the court dispenses with her punishment), thereby relieving the reader from the sentimental anxiety that he might otherwise feel and thus allowing the reader to appreciate the humor. The *exordium* also sets up the dramatic monologue that follows: it tells us where and under what circumstances the speaker delivered her crucial oration.

The *narratio* (setting forth the facts) begins as the speech opens, with Polly Baker describing her predicament. ("I am a poor unhappy Woman . . . deviate in your Sentence from the Law, in my Favour.") Then she advances a *partitio* (a statement of what she hopes to accomplish by her speech): "All I humbly hope is, that your Honours wou'd charitably move the Governor's Goodness on my Behalf, that my Fine may be remitted." After supplying more of the pertinent information (continuing the *narratio*: "This is the Fifth Time . . . for want of Money to pay those Fines"), she begins the *amplificatio* (the arguments proving her case): "This may have been agreeable to the Laws . . . a Power somewhere to dispense with the Execution of them." But before concluding the double syllogism (which begins "But since Laws"), she gives another *partitio*, which says that she will attempt nothing less than to prove that "this Law . . . is . . . unreasonable in itself." This inclusive and fundamental goal supersedes the first, modest *partitio*; and Polly immediately adds another secondary *partitio* ("and particularly severe with regard to me"). Her *amplificatio* or proof continues with an ethical argument ("who have always lived an inoffensive Life") and with the philoprogenitive argument ("in a new Country that really wants People . . . Praise worthy, than a Punishable Action"). She makes a short *refutatio* (replying to the possible arguments against her position): "I have debauch'd no other Woman's Husband, nor inticed any innocent Youth: These Things I never was charged with." Then she relates the first digression. She says that she would prefer to be married, that she has always been willing to marry, but that she was betrayed by her first lover. ("Nor has any one the least cause of Complaint against me . . . advanced to Honour and Power, in the same Government that punishes my Misfortunes with Stripes and Infamy.") After this long *digressio*, she advances another refutation, arguing that if she has committed a religious offense, it should be left to a religious punishment. ("I shall be told, 'tis like. . . . What need is there, then, of your additional Fines and Whippings?") She then proves with a long *amplificatio* that her crime cannot be a religious sin, for God has joined with her in the creation of the children. ("I own, I do not think as you do. . . . I am no Divine.")

Returning to the argument of her primary *partitio* (that "This Law . . . is unreasonable in itself"), she contends that the law turns "natural and useful Actions into Crimes" by promoting abortions and driving "distress'd Mothers" to kill their own "helpless Offspring." ("But if you, great Men . . . expung'd for ever from your Books.") Note that this argument, unique to the *Maryland Gazette* text, is the major "proof" for Polly Baker's primary *partitio*—a *partitio* given twice in each text. As I have suggested, good reasons exist for omitting the passage concerning the murder of infant bastards for some audiences, but there can be no doubt that the argument is a natural and logical part of the speech. At the end of this *amplificatio,* Polly anticipates the peroration, rising to a minor rhetorical climax: " 'Tis the Law, therefore, 'tis the Law itself that is guilty of all these Barbarities and Murders. Repeal it then, Gentlemen; let it be expung'd for ever from your books." Then, before the conclusion, Polly inserts the second *digressio,* returning the satire from its Juvenalian tone back to the Horatian: she urges that a law force bachelors "either to Marry, or pay double the Fine of Fornication every Year." ("And on the other hand . . . if they do their Duty without them?") She concludes the digression with a proof of pathos ("What must poor young Women do"), before rising to the climax: "Yes, Gentlemen, I venture to call it a Duty." Note that the beginning of the *peroration,* which adds a rhetorical flourish to the conclusion, is present only in the *Maryland Gazette* text. In the *peroration,* she calls upon the Bible to support her position (and profession!) before ending with a second allusion to Swift's *Modest Proposal*: she "ought . . . instead of a Whipping, to have a Statue erected to my Memory." Thus this travesty of a classical oration begins with an *exordium* and a *narratio,* progresses through secondary and primary *partitios,* contains *amplificatios, refutatios,* and *digressios,* and concludes with a *peroration.*

It is a critical commonplace that the *Modest Proposal,* like several of Swift's other works, uses the oration as a structural model. Why did he do so? And why did Franklin use the form in his Speech of Polly Baker? The oration was a formula that all educated persons were familiar with in the eighteenth century, and therefore the writer could—as Franklin and Swift did—increase the reader's pleasure by playing with the expectations of the form. In addition, the order of the arguments and their logic may either burlesque the form (as Swift and especially Franklin do) or may reinforce it. In either case, using the form asks the reader to apply his critical skills (practiced upon classical orations and commencement debates throughout his school years), and thus deliberately invites a critical reading. The few sophisticated eighteenth-century readers such as the Abbé Reynal who were taken in by the speech and supposed it real, ignored this critical warning. Although evidence for the reactions of eighteenth-century readers is scant, we know that Silas Deane (of Connecticut) tried to convince the Abbé Reynal that it was a hoax before Franklin owned up that he had created it.[26] "L. Americanus" in the *Gentleman's Magazine* for June 1747 called the Speech "fictitious"; and a writer in the same magazine in August 1781 asked "who was the author of this ingenious composition?" We know that Joel Barlow used it as a touchstone for a hoax: "Accounts like this put one in mind of Dr. Franklin's romance of Mary Baker, so religiously believed and copied by the Abby Raynal."[27] And we know that when the Philadelphia *Independent Gazette* of April 27, 1782, reprinted the Speech, the editor noted that it was "calculated to excite Merriment," thus warning the readers that it was a hoax. Although it appeals to our own vanity to know that some readers in the eighteenth, nineteenth, and twentieth centuries were so foolish as to have supposed that the speech was actually made by some prostitute named Polly Baker, there seems to me little doubt that almost all sophisticated readers would have recognized the Speech of Polly Baker as a mock oration, and would have delighted in the mock ethical arguments, the long digressions, the false logic, and the other characteristics of the mock oration.[28] And Franklin adds to the humor by having a supposedly unlearned prostitute deliver in her own defense a classical oration.

The attentive reader may have noticed (and been impatient at my circumlocutions) the large number of generic terms which I have used to refer to "The Speech of Miss Polly Baker"—*hoax, satire* (*Horatian* and *Juvenalian*), *joke, jeu d'esprit, speech, mock-oration,* and *burlesque.* The reader may have muttered to himself, "Doesn't that fool Lemay know enough to distinguish a *jeu d'esprit* from a satire? Doesn't he know the terms are contradictory?" The diction, I reply, is deliberate. The question of the Speech's genre may be approached by identifying the themes, tone, and authorial voice. The ultimate mode of the literary work—assuming always that it is a successful work of art—will be revealed by the basic themes and by the ultimate authorial voice. Let us approach the subtle question of the ultimate authorial voice by considering first the characteristics of Polly Baker herself.

Polly Baker begins with a humble apology in a modest and reasonable tone, but soon becomes carried away with her argument. She changes her goal (*partitio*) as the speech progresses, from a timid desire to have her fine remitted, to a passionate demand that the law itself be repealed, because its underlying principles are wrong. As she talks, she becomes vehement and proud, revealing that she is convinced not only that she is innocent of any crime but also that she is morally superior—even to her judges. At the end, her passion betrays her supreme vanity. Perhaps the most surprising characteristic of the tone (I use the usual definition of *tone* as the attitude of the speaker toward the subject) is that it is wholly serious. Polly Baker's tone is one of passionate commitment. The long passage on the murder of bastard children ("w"), unique to the *Maryland Gazette* text, is perfectly in keeping with the persona and tone of the fictive Polly Baker, as well as with the diction and syntax of the rest of the speech.[29] But the voice of Franklin behind the speaker—

as I shall attempt to show below—appears first to be humorous, but is finally skeptical, cynical, and even despairing. And yet Franklin evidently felt that the obvious morals found in the Speech were one aspect of the truth.[30]

The positions argued by the persona, Polly Baker, are relatively straightforward. She defends having children (in or out of wedlock). She believes in philoprogenitiveness, like Mandeville, Swift, and Franklin.[31] As a Christian, she believes that God gives infants "rational and immortal souls." She echoes the prevailing belief in scientific deism when she says that the "admirable Workmanship in the Formation of their Bodies" reveals the existence and help of God in their creation. Polly argues that prostitution is no sin unless one debauches some "other Woman's Husband" or entices some "innocent Youth." She protests not only the double standard ("I must Complain of it as unjust and unequal") but also the differing codes of behavior for the two sexes ("What must poor young Women do, whom Custom has forbid to solicit the Men"). She argues for the separation of church and state. Morality and law should be separate ("If mine, then, is a religious Offence, leave it, Gentlemen, to religious Punishments"). She directly attacks New England's blue laws, and she argues that it is only the law that makes the crime ("abstracted from the Law, I cannot conceive . . . what the Nature of my Offence is"). Nearly all of these positions (the exceptions are the belief in souls and the defense of prostitution) are directly advocated by Franklin in his writings. Insofar as we recognize and grant that these are subjects of the Speech, we are admitting that the Speech is a satire.

It is also a *jeu d'esprit*. The obvious authorial voice is comic, thus reassuring the reader that the world is not so bad, that the subjects being satirized are foibles—rather than fundamental human traits—and that the work is, if a satire, a Horatian satire. My students laugh when I read the title of the Speech to them—and this, I am sure, was also the reaction of most readers in the eighteenth century. The situation could have been deadly serious, but the reversal in the title makes it humorous. Only those readers who agreed passionately with one or more of Polly's arguments failed to see that the Speech was humorous. The American audience especially would appreciate it, for Americans frequently told and wrote anecdotes concerning New England's blue laws. In a letter of December 11, 1762, Franklin joked with his Connecticut friend Jared Ingersoll about Connecticut's blue laws, especially that colony's "excessively strict Observation of Sunday." In Flanders, "there was plenty of Singing, Fiddling, and Dancing" on Sundays. Franklin ironically commented "I look'd round for God's Judgments but saw no Signs of them," and concluded the paragraph by remarking that it "would almost make one suspect, that the Deity is not so angry at that Offence as a New England Justice."[32] At least one American in 1747 tried to carry further the American humor contained in the Speech of Polly Baker. The pseudonymous "William Smith" identified Polly Baker as the wife of Paul Dudley (a most incongruous choice—and a family name infamous in New England oral satire)[33] and burlesqued the rural practice of "bundling" (my use of this term, like my use of "blue laws," in anachronistic).

In addition to the situational humor, verbal humor abounds in the Speech. The comic authorial voice is perhaps most easily identified by the puns. (Anyone who maintains that Franklin's contemporaries did not realize that the Speech was a joke, must also maintain that these readers did not appreciate even the most obvious puns in the Speech—it is understandable, of course, that a Frenchman such as the Abbé Reynal might miss the verbal humor.)[34] Franklin, to emphasize the puns, places a pause (in the form of a parenthetical statement) after the two most striking ones: "I cannot conceive (may it please your Honours) what the Nature of my Offence is" and "the first Cause of all my Faults and Miscarriages (if they must be deemed such)." Beside these obvious puns, there are other sly bawdy hits that some readers may find me straining too hard after. In the opening sentence, Polly says that she is "hard put to it to get a tolerable living." I believe that the Franklin who at age sixteen wrote that "Women are prime Causes of a great many Male Enormities" (P, I, 19) would have enjoyed writing that a prostitute had it "hard put to" her "to get a tolerable Living." "Want of Money" may pun on "wanton Money," and the five fine children brought "into the world *at* [my italics] the Risque" of her life, suggests *by* her "risqué" life. Including "Fertility" in the catalogue of prudential wifely virtues ("Industry, Frugality, Fertility, and Skill in Oeconomy") humorously clashes with the rest of the catalogue. When Polly argues that she never "Refused an Offer of that Sort," one at first thinks she is saying that she never refused a sexual liaison. When she remarks that "Custom has forbid" women "to solicit the Men," we see a direct reference to her livelihood, gained by soliciting the men. In defying her enemies to say that she "ever wrong'd Man, Woman or Child" by her way of life, she indirectly states that all her customers got their money's worth. And when this voluptuous fertility symbol maintains that she should have a "statue erected to my Memory," we think that she may indeed have had phalluses "erected" in her memory.[35] And finally, the change in the English text of "County" to "Country" ("n") may suggest that the person who first seduced her and who is "now a Magistrate of this Country" (we recall Hamlet, in Ophelia's lap, also punning on "Country matters") is indeed the judge and ruler of her sexual part.

Beside the obvious comic quality, the authorial voice possesses an underlying current of serious satire. One may distinguish between the subjects satirized by the persona and by her creator, Benjamin Franklin. Although the fictive Polly Baker doesn't know that her real crime is fornication, Benjamin Franklin, who himself served as a magistrate for a brief period, knew what she would have been charged with—and we know that he thought fornication, though treated by most people and by the law as shameful, was not. (See Franklin's letter to Priestley, June 7, 1782, quoted above.) While the naive and obtuse Polly Baker argues that there should be no law against having bastard children, Franklin implicitly argues that there should be no law against fornication, so long as one is not betraying one's partner in marriage or enticing innocent youths. To a degree, Franklin's aims are identical with those of Polly Baker. On legalized prostitution, women's rights, the double standard, blue laws, the separation of church and state, the arbitrariness and rigidity of the law, and on the law itself creating certain crimes—on all of these, Franklin evidently agrees with Polly Baker. But in some ways Franklin goes beyond his persona, and in others he ridicules her.

When the fictive Polly Baker brings up the double standard for men and women, Franklin also touches upon the double standard for the rich and the poor. Polly Baker innocently pleads for herself because she has "no money to fee the lawyers" to plead for her. She complains that it is "unjust and unequal" that her influential first lover "should be advanced to Honour and Power" while she is punished. Franklin, like his readers, knew that the poor were commonly unable to make effective pleas for themselves, while the rich and influential would often not be brought to trial—or if brought to trial, frequently escaped justice by hiring the best legal talent. As he wrote in *Poor Richard* for 1734, "*Laws* like to *Cobwebs* catch small Flies / Great ones break thro' before your eyes."[36]

At three places in the Speech, Franklin (though not his persona) appeals to the commonplace eighteenth-century beliefs in "nature" and in "natural law" as the true standards of justice. Thus when Polly asks if it can be a crime "in the Nature of Things I mean" to have children when the country wants and needs them, Franklin goes behind the ostensible argument of Polly Baker and appeals to the reader's belief in—or at least his familiarity with—the concept of natural law. He repeats the appeal to natural law when Polly asks the "*Gentlemen of the Assembly, then in Court*" not to "turn natural and useful Actions into Crimes, by your prohibitions." And Franklin appeals to nature and to natural law again when he says (in the long passage unique to the *Maryland Gazette*) that the law drives mothers "to imbrue, contrary to Nature, their own trembling Hands in the Blood of their helpless Offspring! Nature would have induc'd them to nurse it up with a Parent's Fondness." In all these cases, Polly ostensibly argues only a specific example—but Franklin expects his readers to recognize the basis for a general appeal to nature and to natural law. Franklin did not himself believe in such cant as the appeal to nature and to natural law, but he expected most of his readers to recognize these commonplaces of Enlightenment thought. And he expected some readers to perceive his satire of these notions.

When Polly Baker triumphantly concludes that she has done the duty "of the first and great Command of Nature, and of Nature's God, *Increase and multiply*," she argues for a philoprogenitiveness that Franklin believed in. But Franklin (though not Polly Baker) also mocks biblical proofs and ridicules those persons who believe in applying every portion of the Bible to life. In this instance, he embodies a major aspect of deistic propaganda (ridicule of the Bible) in his hoax. Franklin also slyly satirizes ministers: when he equates them with magistrates ("Minister, or the Justice"), when he suggests that they perform their duties solely for money (they have lost Polly Baker's marriage fee), when he implies that the loss of these paltry fees would make the ministers (and justices) angry with Polly, and when he has Polly Baker apologize for her ridiculous essay into theology by saying "I am no Divine." The arguments of the ministers, Franklin insinuates, are no better than Polly's in their absurd logic and in the source of their proof.[37]

Franklin, but not his persona Polly Baker, satirizes the most popular eighteenth-century proof for the existence of God—the teleological or design argument. According to the teleological argument, the regularity and order of nature reveals that it was created by a supremely intelligent being. (This, of course, is a basic assumption of scientific deism.) Polly Baker uses this argument when she asks, "But how can it be believed that Heaven is angry at my having Children, when, to the little done by me towards it, God has been pleased to add his divine skill and admirable Workmanship in the Formation of their Bodies, and crown'd it by furnishing them with rational and immortal Souls?" If one believes the teleological argument (and/or if one believes that human beings have souls), then Franklin (who tells in the *Autobiography* of his delight as a youth in using the Socratic method of argument)[38] has cleverly trapped the reader. Logically, he must concede that Polly Baker is right. But, as I have already noted, the same argument would justify rape. Franklin's use of the teleological argument burlesques it, and he must have slyly enjoyed the clever diction in the opening clause, "But how can it be believed."

In passing, Franklin ridicules the cosmological or aetiological argument for the existence of God—which maintains that the universe is an effect which must have a cause. The absent magistrate who originally seduced Polly is called the "first Cause." But Franklin's major religious satire in the speech is based upon theodicy. Franklin ridicules the ideas of God's goodness and omnipotence in view of the existence of evil in the world. As he testified in a letter of June 27, 1763, Franklin considered

unanswerable the question asked by Robinson Crusoe's man Friday:
"Why God No kill the Devil?" (P, X, 303). Polly Baker complains of the
injustice in the fact that the "first Cause . . . should be advanced to Honor
and Power, in the same Government that punishes my Misfortunes with
Stripes and Infamy." Literally, the "first Cause" is her former fiancé who
impregnated and jilted her. But Franklin, for whom religion was always
a favorite subject of satire,[39] also meant the perceptive reader to think of
the standard "first Cause"—God. Franklin's complaint—though not Polly's
—says that if God is All-powerful and all-knowing—if God is either directly, or indirectly but ultimately, responsible for everything that happens—then it is God, the "first Cause," that is the "Betrayer and Undoer"
of man. God is therefore the cause of "all" man's faults. Franklin points
out that it is "unjust and unequal" that God "should be advanced to
Honor and Power" in the opinion of any man who finds any evil in the
World. The ultimate religious satire maintains that if men really believe
in an all-powerful God—then God should be regarded by men as the
cause of evil and of their sinful nature. . . . But Franklin knows that men
believe what they want to believe and that they only use logic to reinforce their wishful desires. As he wrote in the *Autobiography,* "So convenient a thing it is to be a *reasonable* Creature, since it enables one to
find or make a Reason for everything one has a mind to do."[40] Franklin
even introduces a situational joke into the religious satire. Although he
uses the archetypal image of God as the Judge of mankind, God is a
delinquent judge—absent from Court. And, of course, by implication,
absent from the world.

Parallel to the religious satire is Franklin's ridicule of the notions
of natural law and of "following nature." As the above paragraphs imply,
nature and natural law (like the "first Cause" and like the "designs" of
God) are also the "Betrayer and Undoer" of man and are really the causes
of all man's faults. Belief in these notions is as foolish as belief in an
omnipotent and omniscient God. Franklin, a learned naturalist, knew that
nature abundantly justified cannibalism and infanticide. Although his
public writings frequently echo the deistic optimism expressed by Pope
in "whatever is, is right"—his private writings throughout his life (like
the implications of many of his public writings) amply testify to his desire
to change the existing state of affairs, and even to change the nature of
man.[41]

The fictive Polly Baker is Franklin's symbolic representative man.
Her obtuse blindness to her real situation, her passionate conviction of
the justice of her own position, her belief in her absurd and wishful logic,
and especially, her supreme vanity—all characterize human nature, as
Franklin saw it. It is precisely because Polly Baker is, finally, a laughing-
stock that she is Franklin's representative man. When the reader laughs

at Polly Baker's final assertion—that she "ought, in my humble Opinion [as Franklin wrote in the first paragraph of the *Autobiography*, "Indeed I scarce ever heard or saw the introductory Words, *Without Vanity I may say*, &c. but some vain thing immediately followed"], instead of a Whipping, to have a statue erected to my Memory"—he laughs at mankind, and thus he laughs at himself.

The ultimate authorial voice in the Speech is cynical, pessimistic, and even despairing. It is allied thematically with the subtle satire on the nature of man, on the ideas of natural law and the appeal to nature, on the existence of God, and on what mankind's notions of God reveal about the nature of man. But Franklin knows that his eighteenth-century audience (whether English or American) will turn on him for even his relatively acceptable opinions concerning the separation of church and state, the hypocrisy of the double standard, and the defense of fornication—unless the author one-ups the audience by embodying the opinions in a hoax.[42] Further, to safeguard himself from the possible attacks of some outraged persons, Franklin concealed his authorship. When Franklin considered whether or not to make public his religious opinions, he concluded, "He that spits against the Wind, spits in his own Face."[43] But the cynicism, pessimism, and despair of the secondary authorial voice breaks through to the literal, surface-level at one place in the Speech. One passage directly reveals something other than the cheerful, optimistic, and rather shallow Franklin that most readers are conditioned to find. It is the section on mothers murdering their own infants, unique to the *Maryland Gazette* text. This passage completes the Speech, thematically as well as structurally.

Max Hall wrote that this passage "introduced an eye-rolling Polly who is just not the same girl Franklin created" (p. 121). Actually, as I have demonstrated in describing the persona of Polly Baker, the passage dovetails perfectly with the fictive Polly Baker and with the tone. It clashes with the obvious authorial voice. I believe this is what Max Hall meant when he wrote that "this heavy-handed passage does not match the style of the rest of the speech" (p. 121). The style, tone, and persona all match perfectly—but not the comic authorial voice. For the obvious authorial voice in this passage is tragic—disgusted with the law that is responsible for the murders, disgusted with mankind for creating and tacitly supporting such laws, and disgusted with humanity for being capable of murdering even its own children. Although this passage clashes with the usual apparent authorial voice, it is perfectly consistent with the more subtle themes of the Speech and with the underlying authorial voice—but there are those (even some Franklinists!) who are unwilling to recognize that Franklin ever wrote subtle satire.[44]

The question of the genre and of the text of "The Speech of Miss

Polly Baker" finally comes down to a question of the Benjamin Franklin that readers are willing to see. Even without recognizing the Swiftian allusion, the passage on the murder of infant bastards makes the *Maryland Gazette* Speech too Swiftian for the common stereotype of Franklin as a glib, opportunistic, pragmatic optimist. Of course such cant not only ignores the implications of Franklin's major writings, it also denies many straightforward statements: "9 men in 10 are suicides"; "He that best understands the World, least likes it"; "such an inconsiderable nothing as man."[45] In a personal letter to James Logan (too often students ignore Franklin's delicate sense of decorum and of audience), the thirty-one-year-old Franklin even dared to criticize that learned senior stateman's philosophical treatise on the nature of man, saying that it too much ignored the Hobbesian view for the Lockeian.[46] And his letter to Priestley, written at the age of seventy-six, reaffirms his early (and, I believe, consistently held) view of mankind. He wrote that the more he saw of men, "the more I am disgusted with them." And in a macabre tone he even suggested that Priestley might come to regret having murdered "so many honest harmless mice" in his experiments and might come to "wish that, to prevent mischief, you had used boys and girls instead of them."[47]

Many modern readers have found it significant that some previous persons have not realized that the Speech was a hoax; I find it significant that most modern readers have not realized the Speech is ultimately serious. . . . One cannot analyze a work of art too rigorously, but one does deny the unified integrity of the work in dichotomizing its elements. The separate strains of the dichotemization should finally be useful to an appreciation of the whole. If we focus on the persona and tone, the Speech is generally a Horatian satire; if we pay attention primarily to the obvious comic authorial voice, the Speech is a *jeu d'esprit* or a hoax; and if we analyze the implied themes and the underlying authorial voice, the Speech is a bitter Juvenalian satire. But I hope that I have demonstrated that—at least in the *Maryland Gazette* text—"The Speech of Miss Polly Baker" is really all of these at once—a rich example of the intricate but unified literary art of Benjamin Franklin, as well as a splendid example of his extraordinarily complex, skeptical mind.

NOTES

1. Max Hall, *Benjamin Franklin and Polly Baker: The History of a Literary Deception* (Williamsburg, Va.: The Institute of Early American History and Culture, 1960), prints the *General Advertiser* text, as well as the substantive differences of seven other eighteenth-century texts (including the *Maryland Gazette*) and two modern texts, pp. 157–67. Hall omitted, however, one substantive (note "ad" below) and slightly changed one (in "u" below). Hall also

compiled a "Chronological List of Printed Texts of Polly Baker's Speech," pp. 168–77, to which can be added one in the *Boston Gazzette*, March 17, 1760, p. 2; one in the Philadelphia *Independent Gazeteer*, April 27, 1782, p. 2; one in *Beers's Almanac and Ephemeris . . . for 1794* (Hartford: Hudson and Goodwin [1793]), Evans 25152; and *The Speech of Miss Polly Baker* (Danbury, Conn.: J. Crawford, 1797), Huntington Library accession no. 380469. Evans 35007 records from an advertisement in the *Carlisle* [Penna.] *Gazette* for October 19, 1796, that *The Western Almanac for . . . 1797* (Carlisle: Printed for Archibald London by George Kline [1796])—no copy extant—also reprinted the Speech of Polly Baker. And a late-eighteenth-century manuscript version is in the Hastings Papers at the Huntington Library. Although I sometimes differ with Hall on details and interpretations, I am greatly indebted to the splendid research in his enjoyable book. Hall tells the story of his interest in Polly Baker in "An Amateur Detective on the Trail of B. Franklin, Hoaxer," *Proceedings of the Massachusetts Historical Society*, 84 (1972), 26–43. In addition to the article by Albert Matthews cited in note 33 below, I have come across two nineteenth-century notes on Polly Baker not mentioned in Hall's "Alphabetical List of Works Containing Speech or Mentioning Polly," pp. 177–84. They are Sidney Smith Rider's refutation of John Morley's charge that Franklin did not write the Speech, "Notes," *The Nation*, 27 (Nov. 7, 1878), 285; and J[ames] H[ammond] T[rumbull]'s "Miss Polly Baker's Speech," ibid., 27 (Dec. 26, 1878), 398–99, further refuting Morley.

I should also record that G[eorge] P. P[hiles], in a manuscript in the Rare Book Division (call no. °°K.13.11) of the Boston Public Library and in an article in the (Philadelphia) *Evening Bulletin* for Saturday, December 23, 1899 (written by "Penn," which was evidently the pseudonym of William Perrine) claims that a version of *The Speech of Miss Polly Baker* was printed in London by R. Baldwin, Jr., in 1747, "one month before" its publication in the *Gentleman's Magazine* (where it appeared in April 1747). This version, which is copied into the manuscript at the Boston Public Library, would be—if the original existed—the earliest known printing of the Speech. But many circumstances (including the text itself) suggest that, unless other evidence turns up, no credence can be placed in this supposed edition. I can find no reference to this pamphlet in either the *London Magazine* or the *Gentleman's Magazine's* lists of current publications, nor in the most likely library catalogues. And I fear that the dubious reputation of Philes (see Harry Miller Lydenberg, "George Philes: Bookman," *Papers of the Bibliographical Society of America*, 48 [1954], 1–48) will not permit one to believe his unsupported statements.

2. *The Papers of Benjamin Franklin*, ed. Leonard W. Labaree et al. (New Haven: Yale University Press, 1959–), III, 120–25. Hereafter references to this monumental edition are indicated by the initial "P."

3. Max Hall devotes an interesting chapter, pp. 114–25, to the source of the *General Advertiser* text, speculating that Franklin may have sent the Speech to William Strahan or to Peter Collinson, or that one of Franklin's Philadelphia friends might have sent it to an English acquaintance.

4. P, VI, 114–17, lists six (including the copy to "Small") known mid-eighteenth-century texts of the "Parable against Persecution" and discusses the major variations among the several undoubtedly authentic texts of this hoax. And Franklin's essay on religious bigots (written in the form of a letter to Joseph Huey, June 6, 1753) survives in numerous eighteenth-century copies

and transcripts; the editors of the *Papers* report that they "have photostats of ten and could have had more" (P, IV, 503). As I will point out below, textual note "k" suggests that the *General Advertiser* version contains an error in transcription.

5. Hall, p. 121, condemns the *Maryland Gazette* text as apocryphal because of the passage ("w" below) on mothers murdering their own illegitimate children. I will analyze Hall's objections in detail later. Hall does concede that "when all is considered, however, one cannot feel certain that Franklin did not originate the passage" (p. 123). The editors of the *Papers*, III, 121, follow Hall.

J. F. S. Smeall, " 'Miss Polly Baker's Speech,': An American Text," *North Dakota Quarterly*, 27 (1959), 78–80, printed the *Maryland Gazette* text and roundly condemned, on the basis of its prefatory note, the earlier English text as "derivative" and "edited."

6. For an account of Jonas Green, see my *Men of Letters in Colonial Maryland* (Knoxville: University of Tennessee Press, 1972), pp. 193–212; and for Green's relations with Franklin, see pp. 194–95, 198–99. Additional materials on Green and Franklin are in P, III, 153–54; IV, 326; VII, 277; IX, 388; and XIV, 139. Perhaps the best evidence, however, concerning Green's continuing relations with Franklin is to be deduced from Franklin's account books. In the year that Green published The Speech of Polly Baker, Franklin entered charges against Green's account with him on April 1, May 22, June 2, July 31, August 14 and 21, September 10, October 10, and November 17, 1747. George Simpson Eddy, *Ledger "D" 1739–1747*, vol. 2 of *Account Books Kept by Benjamin Franklin* (New York: Columbia University Press, 1929), p. 65.

7. See the discussion of the text of Franklin's poem "I Sing My Plain Country Joan" (P, II, 352) in my "Franklin and the *Autobiography*: An Essay on Recent Scholarship," *Eighteenth-Century Studies*, 1 (1968), 189–90.

8. Samuel Butler, *Hudibras*, Second Part, Canto II, 11. 403–40, in John Wilders's edition (Oxford: Clarendon Press, 1967), pp. 138–39; Edward Ward, *A Trip to New England* in George Parker Winship, ed., *Boston in 1682 and 1699* (Providence: The John Carter Brown Library, 1905), pp. 40–42, 34; and *Jemmy Twicher's Jests* (Glasgow, 1772), p. 23.

9. George Parker Winship, ed., *The Journal of Madam* [Sarah Kemble] *Knight* (1920; repr. New York: Peter Smith, 1935), p. 34. And see the characterization of Connecticut inhabitants in one of the most popular colonial chapbooks: [Thomas Fleet?]. *At a Court Held at Punch-Hall, in the Colony of Bacchus: The Indictment and Tryal of Sr. Richard Rum . . .* 3rd ed. (Boston: T. Fleet, 1724); Evans 2582.

10. Notably in his letter of December 11, 1762, to Jared Ingersoll of Connecticut, P, X, 175–76, cited below.

11. Herbert Davis, ed., *The Prose Works of Jonathan Swift*, XII (Oxford: Basil Blackwell, 1955), 109.

12. Polly Baker's plea that bachelors be forced to marry or to pay double the fine of fornication every year may echo Swift's sixth "Proof" in the *Modest Proposal*: "Sixthly, This would be a great Inducement to Marriage, which all wise Nations have either encouraged by Rewards or enforced by Laws and Penalties" (Davis, ed., XII, 115). See also Henry Baker's spoof, cited by Hall, pp. 100–3.

13. Hall, p. 124, has pointed out that "as Polly Baker's fame spread, New England tended to become unsavory and ridiculous in the eyes of many readers" and that Franklin must have regretted any harm that his wit had

inflicted on New England's good name. Actually, the reputation of New England as a haven for precise puritans began with the Plymouth Colony emigration, and was a common subject of popular seventeenth-century ballads. See C. H. Firth, ed., *An American Garland* (Oxford: Blackwell, 1915), pp. xxiv–xxvi, 25–34, 41–45. And see above, notes 8 and 9. But The Speech of Polly Baker certainly continued New England's unpleasant reputation. And Franklin, in the pre-Revolutionary years, often defended America from similar slanders (P, XIII, 48).

14. The magisterial survey of rhetoric in the eighteenth and preceding centuries is by Wilbur Samuel Howell, *Logic and Rhetoric in England, 1500–1700* and *Eighteenth Century British Logic and Rhetoric* (Princeton: Princeton University Press, 1956 and 1971). For a concise account of the proofs, see Richard A. Lanham, *A Handlist of Rhetorical Terms* (Berkeley: University of California Press, 1969), pp. 106–7.

15. Aristotle and later rhetoricians also admitted an entirely different category of proofs: those that today would generally, in a legal proceedings, be admitted as evidence (Lanham, pp. 106–7).

16. See, for example, the splendid letter on the effect of the depth of water on ships moving through canals (P, XV, 115–18). For a thorough discussion, see I. Bernard Cohen, *Franklin and Newton* (Philadelphia: American Philosophical Society, 1956).

17. P, V, 524; see also III, 365–76; IV, 9–34.

18. Franklin used syllogistic reasoning in his *Dissertation on Liberty and Necessity* (see P, I, 57–71), but he commented on it in the *Autobiography,* "I doubted whether some Error had not insinuated itself unperceiv'd into my Argument, so as to infect all that follow'd, as is common in metaphysical Reasonings" (*The Autobiography of Benjamin Franklin,* ed. Leonard W. Labaree, et al. [New Haven: Yale University Press, 1964], p. 114). The general Enlightenment contempt for the old logic is anticipated by Francis Bacon and expressed by Samuel Butler, *Hudibras,* First Part, Canto I, 11. 65–80, Wilder, ed., p. 3.

19. The false logic in the early prefaces to *Poor Richard's Almanacs* are good examples.

20. For a convenient listing of the twenty-eight valid topics and ten fallacies of Aristotle's rhetoric, see Lanham, pp. 107–10.

21. According to Thomas Jefferson, Silas Deane believed that the Speech of Polly Baker was a hoax because the Speech maintains that there is a law against bastards: " 'the story of Polly Baker . . . when brought before a court of Massachusetts to suffer punishment under a law, which you cite, for having had a bastard. I know there never was such a law in Massachusetts' " (Paul Leicester Ford, ed., *The Writings of Thomas Jefferson* [New York: Putnam's, 1899], X, 121n.). Hall, pp. 94–99, gives examples of trials for fornication, including Eleonor Kellog's, which was for the fifth time.

22. Chester E. Jorgenson and Frank Luther Mott, eds., *Benjamin Franklin: Representative Selections* (1936; rep. New York: Hill and Wang, 1962), p. 444. The foreign-observer persona was a favorite of the seventeenth and eighteenth centuries, being used commonly not only in the travel literature but also in such belletristic genres as the Oriental letters.

23. Marie Jean Antoine Nicolas de Caritat, Marquis de Condorcet, *Eloge de M. Franklin* (Paris: Chez Pyre, 1791). See his *Oeuvres complètes,* 4 (Brunswick: Chez Vieweg, 1804), 117.

24. Jorgenson and Mott, p. 513.

25. Robert Newcomb, "Benjamin Franklin and Montaigne," *Modern Language Notes*, 72 (1957), 489–91, points out Franklin's source. [Antoine Arnauld and Pierre Nicole], *Logic; or the Art of Thinking* (London: John Taylor, 1693), p. 8, argue that Montaigne was a Pyrrhonist. On Franklin's familiarity with *The Port Royal Logic*, see P, I, 58, and *Autobiography*, p. 64. For the divisions of the speech, I follow the terminology given in Lanham, p. 112.

26. Ford, ed., X, 121n. Also cited in Hall, pp. 79–81.

27. *Gentleman's Magazine*, 17 (June 1747), 295; *ibid.*, 51 (August 1781), 367. [Joel Barlow, tr.] J. P. Brissot de Warville, *New Travels in the United States of America* (Dublin: W. Corbet for P. Byrne, 1792), p. 331n. Also cited in Hall, p. 133.

28. For a discussion of one subgenre of the mock-oration, see George Mayhew, "Swift and the Tripos Tradition," *Philological Quarterly*, 45 (1966), 85–101. Even the radical Peter Annet, who wanted to believe in the actuality of the Speech, realized that some people thought the Speech was a hoax: "This story is attested for truth, but whether true or no, the reasons that follow are true." Note "a" in [Peter Annet], *Social Bliss Considered: in Marriage and Divorce* (London: R. Rose, 1749), p. 99.

29. Cf. Hall and the editors of *The Papers of Benjamin Franklin*, cited above, n. 5; and below, cited in the text at length.

30. Franklin probably felt about The Speech of Polly Baker as he did about one of his other great hoaxes, the "Parable against Persecution." He said of the "Parable" that it was "on account of the importance of its moral, well worth being made known to all mankind." At the same time, the "Parable" was a hoax on those "Scripturians" who thought they knew the Bible well. Franklin found their "remarks . . . sometimes very diverting" (Franklin to Benjamin Vaughan, Nov. 2, 1789, in Albert Henry Smyth, ed., *The Writings of Benjamin Franklin* [New York: Macmillan, 1907], X, 53).

In a valuable article, J. F. S. Smeall, "The Readerships of the *Polly-Baker* Texts," *North Dakota Quarterly*, 28 (Winter 1960), 20–29, has also investigated the intent of the Speech, and concluded that the author meant it as a satire "on the marriage customs of the 'Establishment' " (p. 29).

31. Louis A. Landa, "A Modest Proposal and Populousness," *Modern Philology*, 40 (1942), 161–70. Davis, ed., VII, 94–95; IX, 15, 129; XII, 6, 22, 66, 89–90, 109–18, 135, 309, 310. P, IV, 226–34; VI, 225, 475; VIII, 286; IX, 175. And see Alfred Owen Aldridge, "Franklin as Demographer," *Journal of Economic History*, 9 (1949), 25–44.

32. P, X, 175–76. See also note 9, above.

33. William Smith, "Story of Polly Baker No Fiction," *Gentleman's Magazine*, 17 (May 1747), 211; reprinted in Hall, p. 35. "William Smith" may not have been an American, but he must have been someone familiar with American oral humor. For Joseph Dudley (1647–1720) in the oral tradition, see P, I, 78. Albert Matthews has also commented on William Smith's spoof: "A Yarn about Paul Dudley," *Publications of the Colonial Society of Massachusetts*, 28 (1930–33), 446–49. The classic humorous work on Connecticut also joins satire on the blue laws with a satire on bundling (Samuel A. Peters, *General History of Connecticut* [London: for the author, 1781]). See Samuel Middlebrook, "Samuel Peters: A Yankee Munchausen," *New England Quarterly*, 20 (1947), 75–87.

34. Using logic that I do not understand, the editors of the *Papers* (III,

121) seem to maintain that Jonas Green's text may not be authentic because he did not warn his readers that the Speech was a hoax. But I am confident that Jonas Green, who was famous for his humor, appreciated Franklin's hoax and satire.

35. Polly's status as a fertility symbol is emphasized by those versions of the *Gentleman's Magazine* text that added "by whom she has had fifteen children" to the title of the Speech (Hall, pp. 27–29, 159).

36. P, I, 356. Franklin's maxim rephrases a common proverb. See Burton E. Stevenson, *The Home Book of Proverbs, Maxims and Familiar Phrases* (New York: Macmillan, 1948), p. 1085, no. 7 (cf. p. 1084, no. 13, and p. 1085, no. 3). See also Morris P. Tilley, *A Dictionary of the Proverbs in England in the Sixteenth and Seventeenth Centuries* (Ann Arbor: University of Michigan Press, 1950), L116; and *The Oxford Dictionary of English Proverbs*, 3rd ed., rev. by F. P. Wilson (Oxford: Clarendon, 1970), pp. 446–47. Peter Annet (see above, n. 28), in his notes to an edition of The Speech of Polly Baker, also comments on the implied double standard for the rich and poor (Annet, p. 99, n. "b," and p. 10, n. "q"). Given Franklin's love for proverbs, it may be conjectured that the basic ideas of the Speech are an outgrowth of two proverbs: "Where there is no Law, there can be no Transgression." And "Fornication . . . is no sin." See Hall, pp. 51–52, for two examples of the former. Although it is not included in the *Papers*, I believe that Franklin wrote the address to Samuel Sewall in the *New England Courant*, Feb. 4, 1723, p. 1, which cites this proverb. And Franklin uses it in P, II, 119. For the latter, see Bartlett Jere Whiting, "Proverbs in Cotton Mather's *Magnalia*," *Neuphilologische Mitteilungen*, 73 (1972), 480. For analogues of the latter, see Whiting, *Proverbs, Sentences, and Proverbial Phrases from English Writings Mainly before 1500* (Cambridge: Harvard University Press, 1968), L167 ("Lechery is no sin") and L478 ("Alas! that (ever) Love is sin").

37. A. Owen Aldridge has pointed out that Franklin wrote The Speech of Polly Baker "not long after his struggle with the Presbyterian synod of Philadelphia in which he had damned 'the Impositions of Priests, whether Popish, Presbyterian or Episcopal.' With Polly Baker he was still letting loose his anticlerical animus" (Aldridge, *Benjamin Franklin and Nature's God* [Durham: Duke University Press, 1967], p. 134).

38. *Autobiography*, pp. 64–65. Hall, p. 111, has suggested that "it is conceivable that the satire of the speech was directed both at the orthodox religionists who wished to impose their own moral ideas on others and the unorthodox who were forever appealing to Nature."

39. In an "Apology for Printers" (which was occasioned by his printing a lampoon on the clergy), Franklin stated, "I never write or talk against the Clergy my self." But he added, "Some have observed that 'tis a fruitful Topic, and the easiest to be witty upon of all others" (P, I, 198). Aldridge, *Benjamin Franklin and Nature's God*, shows that religion was a major subject of Franklin's writing throughout his life. In his *Dissertation on Liberty and Necessity* (1725), the nineteen-year-old Franklin wrote: *"Unde Malum?"* has been long a Question, and many of the Learned have perplex'd themselves and Readers to little Purpose in Answer to it" (P, I, 59). Franklin's consideration of theodicy in the *Dissertation* follows directly after his definition of God, the "First Mover," as "all-wise, all-good, all powerful."

40. *Autobiography*, p. 88. For a brief but interesting examination of the role of reason in Franklin's thought, see Gerald Stourzh, *Benjamin Franklin*

and American Foreign Policy (1954; repr. Chicago: University of Chicago Press, 1969), pp. 13–15. Franklin also avowed the impossibility of reconciling things as they actually are with the "establish'd Doctrine of the Goodness and Justice of the great Creator" in a letter to his favorite sister, Jane Mecom, in 1770 (P, XVII, 315–16; cf. P, II, 119, and XVIII, 185).

41. See Stourzh, pp. 10–12, for remarks on Franklin's attitudes toward "Cosmic Toryism."

42. Franklin frequently employed a similar rhetorical strategy in writing American propaganda for an anti-American audience. The best known of such satires are "An Edict by the King of Prussia" and "Rules for Reducing a Great Empire to a Small One."

43. P, VII, 294. In the eighteenth century, ostensibly personal letters were commonly used for essays (i.e., for discussions of selected topics), as well as for personal communications. This "letter" is really not a personal communication, but a discussion of whether one should reveal and promulgate heterodox religious opinions.

44. Because the current editors of the *Papers* think that the irony in the splendid hoax "The Captivity of William Henry" is "in some places . . . almost too subtle and indirect," they doubt Franklin's authorship of the satire, despite overwhelming evidence (P, XV, 145–48).

45. P, III, 346 (*Poor Richard*, October 1749); P, IV, 405 (*Poor Richard*, June 1753); P, I, 102.

46. P, II, 184–85.

47. June 7, 1782, in Smyth, 8:453.

PART III

Franklin in Retrospect

John Griffith

❧ Franklin's Sanity and the
Man behind the Masks

Franklin is in some ways a most representative man, perhaps the closest thing we have to being the ordinary man's philosopher and a spokesman for sense that is genuinely common. Yet because of this, paradoxically, the reasons for which we read him are quite uncommon and extraordinary. From paragraph to paragraph, his prose is solid but not startling; sensible but seldom profound. With the possible exception of the *Autobiography* (and passing objective judgment on that is about as difficult now as passing judgment on the Declaration of Independence), none of his writings, taken by itself, is indisputably a literary masterpiece. To really appreciate the stature of his written achievement, one must read him at length—his essays and treatises and public and private letters. For, whether as his admirers or as his critics, what we read him for is his sanity. And sanity, like accuracy in a clock, becomes apparent only over the long haul.

This makes Franklin a notable oddity among the major American writers (whether or not he is a great writer, I trust no one will deny that he is a major one). We do not cherish Edwards or Poe or Melville or Hawthorne or Thoreau or Hemingway or Faulkner for their *sanity*—unless of course we have a special point to make about what it means to be sane. But with Franklin, whether we speak of his worldly good sense and admire him for it, or of his canny simple-mindedness and cheerful ignorance of the human depths, and resent him for it, it is, generally speaking, his sanity that we notice when we read him.

Why should mere good sense be a reason for reading an author dead almost two centuries (apart, that is, from his special value for professional historians)? Unembellished good sense in a contemporary writer is one thing; we may value contemporary critics or social commentators because of the way their good judgment clarifies issues which are still being decided. But that hardly explains why one should take an interest in Franklin's sensible comments on issues which, in their literal form, haven't been vital for a century or more. Just making sense is, almost by definition, an undistinguished thing to do; highly wrought strangeness is a much more interesting literary virtue.

Yet Franklin's works do continue to attract interest. Much of it, of course, derives from his historical importance. Being both a Founding Father and an indispensable commodity in academic courses on American thought and letters, he has a considerable audience on those grounds alone. But beyond that, I believe that for many readers there is at the heart of Franklin's work a mystery, as enigmatic in its way as Thoreau's sensual asceticism is in its, or Faulkner's despairing exuberance. To read Franklin at length and with real attention is to have one's imagination stirred by the sense of something unique and not wholly explicable going on between and behind the lines.

I venture to say that this mystery grows out of the impression Franklin gives of being so completely in control of things: of his language, his reasoning, his audience, and himself. Not that he reveals a compulsive need for control or a tense fastidiousness like Irving's or Poe's or Hemingway's; the mind that lives in Franklin's prose is peculiarly sure of itself, and at ease. It is not just coherent and rational; it is also unworried, and unthreatened. The ghosts of his adversaries or his personal memories plague him very little. The *Autobiography* confesses that this easy manner is actually the product of laborious self-training and calculation. But the confession does not explain the quality away. It remains the most generally intriguing aspect of Franklin's written legacy.

It may seem odd to call a simple air of calmness and control intriguing and mysterious, as if it needed some special explanation. With at least one part of our minds, even in the chaotic twentieth century, we tend to think of regulation and serenity as the ordinary conditions of human life; we operate on the assumption that, unless something catastrophic happens to make us lose control, we automatically have it. Franklin usually wrote as if that were the basic truth. "The Way to Wealth, if you desire it, is as plain as the Way to Market," he told the famous Young Tradesman. And in the *Autobiography* he declared, "I have always thought that one Man with tolerable Abilities may work great Changes, and accomplish great Affairs among Mankind, if he first forms a good Plan, and . . . makes the Execution of that Plan his sole Study and Business."[1] "If Passion drives, let Reason hold the Reins," says Poor Richard. Indeed, we say; that's good advice.

But we have another side which recognizes that this air of good sense and easy control, far from being the fundamental condition of life, is an utter fabrication. This side perceives that the power to be at ease and in command of oneself and one's surroundings is in fact a superhuman feat, and that St. Paul spoke for more than himself when he said, "I can will what is right, but I cannot do it. For I do not do the good I want, but the evil I do not want is what I do" (Romans 7:18–19). Hence, the easy Franklin manner intrigues us. As we read, we think, "Yes, of course, this is obvious, this is only natural"—and at the same time we wonder, "How does he carry it off? How does he keep the illusion of omnicompetence going so effortlessly?"

From this simultaneous acceptance and doubt has grown up a lingering conception of Franklin as a man of mystery, the secret springs of whose behavior will perhaps never be fully seen. We have come to look on his life and writing as, in a peculiar way, *performances*; and we see in his character, both literary and historical, the fundamental elements of both stage actor and confidence man. How else, the logic seems to go, could he have appeared so utterly sane?

Franklin himself provided the first suggestions that his life was to be understood as something other than simply a life, spontaneous and unrehearsed. He sometimes described himself as, in effect, his own impresario. In 1756 he wrote to George Whitefield, "Life, like a dramatic Piece, should not only be conducted with Regularity, but methinks it should finish handsomely. Being now in the last Act, I begin to cast about for something fit to end with."[2] His "character" or reputation was to him almost a commodity, to be cultivated, maintained, and invested. When Richard Jackson invited him to take part in sponsoring settlements in Nova Scotia, Franklin's reply is a case in point: "Since there is no likelihood of my being engag'd in any Project of a new Government, the Popular Character I have in America may at least be of Use in procuring Settlers for some Part under an old one."[3]

The disgruntled John Adams, who chafed at Franklin's coolly developed social manner, spoke of him and Voltaire as "two aged actors upon this great theatre of philosophy and frivolity" when they dramatically embraced amid the cheers of the French Academy in 1778.[4] In *Israel Potter*, Melville remarked that, "having carefully weighed the world, Franklin could act any part in it. . . . His mind was often grave, but never serious. At times he had seriousness—extreme seriousness—for others, but never for himself."[5]

As scholars and commentators have gone over the Franklin canon more and more closely, the theme has solidified, that Franklin characteristically engaged in pretending to be someone he really wasn't quite. The *Autobiography* confesses that Franklin's standard was not so much *truth* as *usefulness*. And this observation, whether advanced by himself, by one of his attackers, or by one of his defenders, inevitably casts unsteadying shadows on his sincerity.

The theme appears almost equally among favorable and unfavorable commentaries. D. H. Lawrence protests, "I still believe that honesty is the best policy," as Franklin taught him; but "I dislike policy altogether."[6] "To raise the question of the relation between Franklin's public and private personality, and of the character and integrity of his procedure, is difficult," says Gladys Meyer, "because Franklin was discreet and always aware of the public to whom he spoke, if and when he revealed himself at all. His biography, seemingly so candid, is a masterpiece of discretion. He had no intimate friend, letters to whom might give any direct clue to his inner spirit."[7] Carl Becker observes, "In spite of his ready attention to the business in hand, there is something casual about his efficient dispatch of it; he manages somehow to remain aloof, a spectator still, with amiable curiosity watching himself functioning effectively in the world."[8] Wheeling his printer's supplies through the streets in a wheelbarrow, says Carl Van Doren, "was the first of the roles that Franklin strategically assumed as he was to assume others later. For his character was never of one single piece, like, for example, Washington's. Franklin's was rich, flexible, dramatic."[9] "Everything he did he gave his best to, and most everything he did he did well, but behind the gestures and routines of his participation was always a reserve, a certain ironic sense which took amusement as well as satisfaction from experience," says Robert Sayre. "This was the actor in him. . . . The man behind the actor was always bigger than the single part."[10] Max Farrand has praised "his ability to take a detached, impersonal, dispassionate point of view," especially toward his own doings, which he could observe and record "with complete detachment of self."[11] Theodore Hornberger has written that Franklin was a man "whose character remains mysterious" behind "voluminous writings [which] are full of what he himself regarded as tricks of his trade."[12] And J. H. Plumb has most recently pronounced: "Throughout his life he was busy manufacturing a *persona* which he hoped would appeal not only to his own time and generation but also to the future."[13]

This general view of Franklin is dominated by a kind of large metaphor or myth: "the man behind the masks." Simplified and brutally extracted from the often very sophisticated and intelligent contexts in which it figures, it goes something like this: Once upon a time, in the 1710s and 1720s, there was Benjamin Franklin, a natural, spontaneous, uncomplicated youth, clearly visible to anyone in Boston or Philadelphia who bothered to look at him as he boisterously made his way—working, writing poetry, carousing with his friends, arguing with his brother, "hurrying into intrigues with low women." As he grew older, a change took place in this natural Franklin, more or less gradually. He began to develop a sense of purpose, even of chicanery some would say, as he learned various styles of personal and public rhetoric by which he could control the world around him—through controlling its impressions of himself. He learned to play the reasonable, open-minded thinker, and the industrious, sober, reliable tradesman; he learned to find the men whose friendship would pay off in trade and politics, and he arrogated that friendship by acting the character those men would appreciate. Gradually or suddenly, the true, natural Franklin disappeared behind a variety of thoughtfully constructed masks (the number would grow as his performances moved onto an international stage). From then on, his character had to be understood as a complex of identities: the identities he had learned (the worldly, public ones, but also the relatively private ones he showed to his friends and family), behind which lurked the real Franklin, a cautious, secretive, perhaps (this depends on one's point of view) even a sinister inner man, who controlled the actions of the visible Franklin like a puppeteer or a Madison Avenue advertising expert intent on selling his product by creating a pleasing image of it.

This may exaggerate the outlines of the myth somewhat—although one reads versions of it which are hardly more sharply pointed than mine (as, for instance, when William Hanna writes that Franklin was a "skilled manipulator" who "worked hard to fashion an influential personal instrument especially suited to the small, intimate society of Philadelphia" by "[correcting] or [disguising] what he thought were flaws in his personality.")[14] But if it is an exaggeration, it can still be helpful, for this reason: since, as seems entirely likely, the myth of the man behind the masks is a permanent part of the discussion of Franklin and his writings, the moral and psychological implications of that myth are worth considering explicitly. This is especially important in light of the fact that the idea of behavior as role-playing has in our day become a central, even fashionable one. At its most elaborate it is the basis for comprehensive psychological and philosophical systems (such as Kenneth Burke's philosophy of dramatism, for example, and the psychological school of transactional analysis, exemplified in popular handbooks like *Games People Play*); more simply it has served as an image for the spiritual alienation threatening the modern psyche (as when Eliot's J. Alfred Prufrock in his torpor laments, "There will be a time to prepare a face to meet the faces that you meet"). Inevitably, the general interest in role-playing affects the modern reader's reaction to the role-playing elements in Franklin.

It raises both moral and psychological questions: Is Franklin's role-playing strictly honest? Is it good for one's spiritual or psychological well-being? And it raises questions of historical applicability: Can Franklin's sense of himself as a performer be fairly described in terms growing out of the very different historical situations of the nineteenth and twentieth centuries? These are large, loose questions, difficult to answer conclusively. But they are unavoidable aspects of the Franklin myth.

The moral question is perhaps the most easily disposed of. Playing a role, like speaking a language, is in itself morally neutral. There is no more inherent dishonesty in playing a social role than there is in speaking words instead of unintelligible instinctive grunts. But, as Erving Goffman points out in *The Presentation of Self in Everyday Life,* it is easy to forget that fact.

> In our own Anglo-American culture there seems to be two
> common-sense models according to which we formulate our
> conceptions of behavior: the real, sincere, or honest performance;
> and the false one that thorough fabricators assemble for us, whether
> meant to be taken unseriously, as in the work of stage actors, or
> seriously, as in the work of confidence men. We tend to see real
> performances as something not purposely put together at all, being
> an unintentional product of the individual's unselfconscious
> response to the facts in his situation. And contrived performances
> we tend to see as something painstakingly pasted together, one
> false item on another, since there is no reality to which the items of
> behavior could be a direct response. It will be necessary to see
> now that these dichotomous conceptions are by way of being the
> ideology of honest performers, providing strength to the show they
> put on, but a poor analysis of it.[15]

Performing, as Goffman calls it—the quite intentional assumption of dramatic roles dictated by one's society—is a constant fact of human life. Learning to play the parts which go to make up one's identity is crucial in letting both the world and yourself know who you are.

No one, I think, with the possible exception of a few extreme mystics who flirt with psycho-suicide, would seriously deny that in a fundamental way the whole process of realizing one's humanity (as distinct from mere organic existence) requires some consciousness of self—that is, a conscious recognition that one is an individual related to but separate from other people and existence generally. A basic difference between a man and an animal is that the man thinks of himself as a self. This, as George Herbert Mead pointed out years ago, means that the man is able to objectify himself, by looking at himself "as an object," the way someone else might look at him. Mead likened the development of self-awareness to the way in which one learns to play a game with other people. A child can of course play by himself—pretending or acting as if he were the teacher or the father or the sheriff, one after another. But when he takes part in a game involving several people—hide and seek, or baseball for instance—he must, in a sense, become all those other people at once: he must imaginatively enter into the points of view of opponents and teammates. "What he does is controlled by his being every-one else on that team, at least in so far as those attitudes affect his own particular response."[16] His sense of self—his understanding of who he is, in the little world of the game—depends upon seeing himself as others see him, and playing the role he is expected to play.

The same process prevails in the more complicated social world. "After all," says Mead, "what we mean by self-consciousness is an awakening in ourselves of the group of attitudes which we are arousing in others, especially when it is an important set of responses which go to make up the members of the community."[17]

Much of Franklin's so-called role-playing, then, is accounted for by the hardly shameful fact that he was more actively aware than most people are of the social process by which self-awareness is formed. His writings are dotted with object lessons in how one learns, adjusts, and improves the *self*, through a consideration of the impact it makes on other people. The *Autobiography* is virtually a paradigm of the healthy, intelli-gent development of this sense of identity. In large part, it is a story of "socialization"—of Franklin's becoming aware of the image he presents to the world, of learning the language and the categories society uses in labeling and dealing with that image, and of learning to assume the best roles available in that society. It is the story of a boy learning to embrace, as the older Franklin put it on looking back, that which is *useful* over that which is merely *true*—a distinction mined with epistemological pit-falls, but suggesting clearly enough Franklin's willingness to lay aside attitudes that might have some direct private appeal, in favor of those that are more generally acceptable and socially productive. In short, it is the story of learning to be approved of—softening one's argumentative manner, correcting or suppressing one's indecorous impulses, and im-pressing other people with one's reliability, industriousness, amicability, and good sense.

There is nothing inherently immoral about this process. Thoreau, to take the example of a man extremely different from Franklin in char-acter and style, played at least as elaborate a set of social roles in his Walden hermitage as Franklin did in his Philadelphia print shop. They are not the *same* roles, and Thoreau does not talk about them with quite the same bland openness that Franklin does (although the beginning of the chapter "Brute Neighbors" in *Walden* shows that Thoreau was sharply aware of the stage characters he was assuming). But they are no less artfully contrived, and no less deeply imbued with what Kenneth Burke calls "the rhetorical motive"—the impulse to make an impression.[18] I'm not concerned here with the relative virtues of the Franklinian and Thoreauvian roles. My point is only that the general notion of playing a role is in itself morally neutral because it partakes of that universal business of self-understanding and expression which is too fundamental for moral distinction.

But even if one accepts this point, he is still faced with a possible objection to Franklin's particular psychology: the objection that, while it may not be wicked, it may not be healthy either.

The suspicions implied in that objection are readily understandable. To the modern reader at least, the inveterate role-player seems to run serious psychological risks. Hendrik M. Ruitenbeek, for example, in *The Individual and the Crowd,* suggests that too much role-playing threatens to shatter the sense of self. For many modern Americans, says Ruitenbeek, "living has almost of necessity become a matter of dividing the personality, of being one man at work, another man at home, a third man in suburban public affairs, a fourth man at the country club. To live out so many and often such contradictory roles would be difficult even for someone who had a secure identity. For a person whose identity is not firmly established, role playing can become even more confusing: the personality tends to become a many-layered covering for a hollow space within; one seeks a core and finds only emptiness."[19]

And it might seem that the problems would multiply rather than diminish to the extent that the person becomes aware that his different identities are, in fact, roles rather than "his true self." A firm self-awareness, founded on a confident mastery of the parts one must play in the world, may be healthy and psychologically steadying—but the added knowledge that those parts are actually a kind of fiction, separable from the "true character" of the actor, presumably has the opposite effect, and tends toward what the modern world calls alienation, the sense that what one *does* is not really true to what one *is.* The self-acknowledged role-player risks having his healthy self-awareness become a painful self-consciousness—a sense of self exacerbated and made vivid by feelings of internal conflict or anxiety.

William James analyzed this spiritual condition in *The Varieties of Religious Experience,* calling it "the divided self" and finding in it a particularly intense kind of mental torment. He quotes the novelist Daudet as an instance of it:

> Homo duplex, homo duplex. The first time that I perceived
> that I was two was at the death of my brother Henri, when my

father cried out so dramatically, "He is dead, he is dead!" While my first self wept, my second self thought, "How truly given was that cry, how fine it would be at the theatre." I was then fourteen years old.

This horrible duality has often given me matter for reflection. Oh, this terrible second me, always seated whilst the other is on foot, acting, living, suffering, bestirring itself. This second me that I have never been able to intoxicate, to make shed tears, or put to sleep. And how it sees into things, and how it mocks.[20]

If our myth of the man behind the masks is at all a valid image of Franklin's psychology, is it possible that he did not to some extent share Daudet's perception of a "terrible second me" sitting unmoved behind the scenes of his own life? How could Franklin abide what was apparently a rather constant self-scrutiny—what Farrand calls "a complete detachment of self"—without suffering the torment James describes? Why did he not feel his identity torn apart into separate, contending voices, like the unhappy youth whose case Erik Erikson quotes: "A voice within him which was disparaging him began to increase at about this time. It went to the point of intruding into everything he did. He said, 'If I smoke a cigarette, if I tell a girl I like her, if I make a gesture, if I listen to music, if I try to read a book—this third voice is at me all the time— "You're doing this for effect; you're a phony." ' "[21]

Is it miraculous that Franklin seems never to have been troubled by this painful, conflict-ridden self-consciousness? One reads his collected writings from end to end without seeing a trace of serious self-doubt, self-loathing, self-anger, or any other radical form of intrapsychic conflict and anxiety. The scattering of acknowledged *errata* in the *Autobiography* are scarcely signs of a man at war with himself—any more than is the "self-scolding" Franklin administers in his "Dialogue between Franklin and the Gout." If anything, Franklin's most dangerous psychological trait (dangerous, that is, from his own point of view, in that it sometimes threatened to interfere with his getting on in the way he wished) was an overabundance of self-satisfaction. The many little strokes of irony which Franklin customarily inflicted on himself for his vanity suggest that virtually his only consistent self-criticism was that he was too satisfied with himself. Clearly enough, this little foible caused him no serious mental distress.

The fact of the matter is that Franklin succeeded in being self-aware without being self-conscious. In his maturity he knew exactly who he was, what he wanted to do, and how to do it, without having to question or analyze his motives.

For the sake of making a point, let me venture a remark that will

at first seem far-fetched: Franklin's sense of self can best be thought of
as a species of mysticism—a kind of American work-ethic folk mysticism.
It is mystical in just this one crucial point: it centers on an essential *loss
of self*—that is, loss of the self which derives from internal conflict.

In his essay "The Ego and Mystic Selflessness," philosopher
Herbert Fingarette has compiled a general description of psychological
attributes shared by great mystics in several religious traditions. Much
of what he says about the mystics' "self-forgetfulness" applies with un-
canny accuracy to Franklin's attitudes.

When the great mystics succeed in "losing the sense of self," says
Fingarette, they do *not* break down, forget who they are, nor suffer
"psychotic-like confusion of 'inner' and 'outer' [realities]"; they fully retain
the ability to distinguish between themselves and the rest of the world.
"The mystic, in the advanced stages of his development, lives in the
world, among 'wine-bibbers and butchers,' and acts effectively in his
relationships with others. This implies that he takes into account his body,
his social situation, his personal qualities, powers and purposes. It is in
just these respects that the self-representations play an essential role, for
they are the psychic perceptions of the person and his powers and purposes. Hence they cannot be the self which the enlightened mystic has
lost."[22] What he has lost is the painful introspective sense of self which
accompanies anxiety. "The introspective 'sense of self' occurs in the context of the *disruption* of 'normal' ego activity," Fingarette writes. "We do
not normally have the *feeling* that our actions and decisions are or are not
ours; we simply act or decide. The normal introspective self-'feelings' are
like the feeling of the air we breathe. *Normally* we neither feel that the air
exists nor that it has ceased to exist. Only when there is trouble do we
become aware of the air" (p. 562).

In certain important psychological respects, then, the mystic's
special power is his ability to maintain the so-called "normal" unself-
consciousness. His drives and motives do not conflict, his sense of himself
is firm and coherent and gives no cause for brooding or lingering self-
analysis, and he can act with unimpaired efficiency.

> The enlightened one is, therefore, not only an unassuming and
> "ordinary" person (as well as an extraordinary one), he is in many
> ways "more ordinary" than most people. He is not overly proud,
> not driven by ambition, not prone to keeping up with the Joneses,
> not given to disingenious logical or theoretical disquisitions. He
> tends to shun words. He suffers, enjoys, knows pain and pleasure,
> but he is not driven or dominated by these. Sensual without being
> sensualist, he is also aware of his ills without being hypochondriacal.
> "He does not call attention to himself. . . .

In the last analysis, then, the mystic way is a "simple" and
"obvious" way—for those who will open their eyes. For the mystic
experience is the achievement of "emptiness," of "nothingness."
That is to say, it is not the achievement of any finally fixed state of
mind or any universal doctrine at all. It is the liberation from
neurotic fixation and dogma of all kinds.   [p. 570]

Reading these words, one is reminded of a multitude of Franklinian
passages: Franklin's thanking God "that he has pleased to give me such a
[reasonable] mind, with moderate Passions, or so much of his gracious
Assistance in governing them; and to free it early from Ambition, Avarice,
and Superstition, common Causes of much Uneasiness to Men."[23] "One's
true Happiness depends more upon one's own Judgement of one's self,
on a Consciousness of Rectitude in Action and Intention, and in the
Approbation of those few who judge impartially, than upon the Applause
of the unthinking undiscerning Multitude, who are apt to cry Hosanna
today, and tomorrow, Crucify him."[24] "I, who am totally ignorant of
military Ceremonies, and above all things averse to making Show and
Parade, or doing any useless Thing that can only serve to excite Envy or
provoke Malice, suffer'd at the Time [when the Pennsylvania militia gave
him a military escort of honor] much more Pain than I enjoy'd Pleasure,
and have never since given an Opportunity for anything of the Sort."[25]
"And Self-denial is neither good nor bad, but as 'tis apply'd: He that
denies a Vicious Inclination is Virtuous in proportion to his Resolution,
but the most perfect Virtue is above all Temptation, such as the Virtue
of the Saints in Heaven."[26]

The mystic in his triumph, like Franklin at his ease, is not overcon-
cerned with explaining himself. Emerging into "the freedom of introspective 'self-forgetfulness' of the psychically unified self," as Fingarette puts
it (p. 564), he does not feel driven or caught or alienated from the
activities he engages in. The fundamental mechanism by which Franklin
achieved this peace of mind—insofar as it was an achievement of active
choice and philosophical decision—was the device of keeping busy.
Aristotle pointed out long ago that happiness is not the purpose of life,
but rather a by-product of living well. Franklin's Poor Richard had the
same psychological point when he said, "Fly Pleasures, and they'll follow
you." Forget about the need for contentment, and you'll be content.
Aldous Huxley has called it the "Law of Reversed Effort." "The harder
we try with the conscious will to do something, the less we shall
succeed."[27]

Franklin knew of "the proneness of human Nature to a life of ease,
of freedom from care and labour."[28] But he knew it was folly to expect
contentment in those conditions. Building a fort at Gnadenhut "gave me

occasion to observe, that when Men are employ'd they are best con-
tented. For on the Days they work'd they were good-natur'd and chearful; and with the consciousness of having done a good Days work they
spent the Evenings jollily; but on the idle Days they were mutinous and
quarrelsome, finding fault with their Pork, the Bread, &c. and in continual
ill-humour; which put me in mind of a Sea-Captain, whose Rule it was
to keep the Men constantly at Work; and when his Mate once told him
that they had done every thing, and there was nothing farther to employ
them about, *Oh*, says he, *make them scour the Anchor*" (*Autobiography*,
p. 234). It is worth recognizing the psychological similarity between this
principle and the mystic's devices of turning the mind away from subjective areas of discontentment or dissatisfaction and toward some higher,
more satisfying object—meditating on texts (this was Jonathan Edwards'
device), or an exalted image of the Church, or the Person of God Himself.
"The education which tradition has ever prescribed for the mystic," says
Evelyn Underhill, "consists in the gradual development of an extraordinary faculty of concentration, a power of spiritual attention . . . a self-
forgetting attentiveness, a profound concentration, a self-merging, which
operates a real communion between the seer and the seen."[29]

Let me hasten to acknowledge that the mysticism I'm attributing
to Franklin is mystical only in this one psychological particular—the
ability to lose self-consciousness in vigorous concentration. Differences in
language, style, tone, and content between his philosophy and classic
mysticism make them in most things polar opposites. And the ecstatic
element in mysticism—those shuddering emotional orgasms in which the
mind is momentarily overwhelmed by the Presence of the Unseen—is
entirely missing from Franklin's experience, so far as I can tell. But the
inner tranquillity that survives the death of the introspective self, the
fundamental sense of innocence and peace in one's heart—these seem to
have been his.

Some Franklin commentators, of course, see his supposed tranquillity as an affectation. They see his almost unbroken introspective
silence as a void, and are tempted to fill it in. "The bitter anger toward
his brother, the sexual hunger of a plain-faced youth, the longing for
intellectual and social acceptance, the unassuageable thrust of ambition,
the rage against the world that any man of great powers must feel at
times of frustration—were these things repressed into the deep recesses
of his being?"[30] They call for psychoanalysis to get to the bottom of
Franklin—for "a Clark or an Erikson" who will give "an adequate psychic
analysis."[31] They assume that Franklin was in fact a driven man (aren't
we all?): "He craved distinction, hungered for success, lusted for money,
and used all his resources—guile, intelligence, and above all, the opportunities of his age—to achieve them."[32] They speculate about whether it

was a lingering Puritanical sense of spiritual guilt,[33] or a more secular "social guilt" that spurred him on.[34]

If a prodigious capacity for working, writing, observing, politicking, and socializing is de facto evidence of a compulsive, driven mind, then there is no denying that Franklin's belongs to the breed. But the premise is shaky. I believe there is a crucial difference between that mind which is in effect the wretched prey of its motives, helplessly caught in the need to expiate imagined guilts or to defend itself against imagined enemies or otherwise to frantically obey private, subjective dictates—and that mind which, like Franklin's, sees objectively and fulfills natural, widely understandable desires. The first of these two minds tends toward neurosis or psychosis; it might be brilliant, but it is also likely to be tense and unhappy. The second is what Fingarette calls "ego-syntonic," a mind happily in agreement with itself, and characterized not by a feeling of helplessness before fixed or insistent impulses, but by a sense of freedom. If this distinction is allowed, then Franklin clearly belongs in the second category.

The conclusion this leads to in the matter of Franklin's role-playing is that we must be careful of modern preoccupations with that element of his psychology. It is perhaps fair to say that Franklin was not so aware of his masks as his commentators have been. Certainly the concept of pretending is less conspicuous in his own remarks than it is in discussions written about him. The myth of the man behind the masks, while it has some limited value as a description of the way it must have felt to *be* Franklin, is probably truer as a description of the way he looks from the outside. "What you would seem to be, be really," said Poor Richard; and I see no reason to doubt that Franklin found this a practicable piece of advice. As the Art of Virtue section of the *Autobiography* shows, Franklin believed that one's character could be calculatedly shaped, through the development of good habits of thought and action. His famous confession that he never achieved the reality of the virtue of humility, although he had a good deal of success with "the *appearance* of it," is really only as damning as we choose to make it. The trouble with humility was that it alone among his thirteen virtues did not spring from his own conception of self-improvement. It alone required an adjustment, not in how he thought about and treated other people and things, but in his attitude *toward himself*. It was, in short, a most un-Franklinian virtue. Franklin obviously had too strong and favorable an opinion of himself to "achieve the *reality*" of humility—that is, a genuinely low regard for himself. When he says he achieved "a good deal with regard to the *appearance* of it," he might as well have said he had succeeded in being humble *to a degree* but not absolutely. He was describing a partially unsuccessful (because halfhearted) attempt at self-improvement, rather than a blatant piece of deception. Certainly as a confession of sharp-eyed slyness, the passage is pretty innocent stuff.

The same quality of innocence prevails in all Franklin's famous "deceptions." If one really considers, for example, the famous scene in the *Autobiography* where Franklin wheels his printer's supplies through the streets so that people will see how industrious he is, one is far more struck by the unself-conscious naiveté of both the wheelbarrow pusher *and the narrator* (who describes this small act of posturing quite without embarrassment—in fact, with a rather boyish pride), than by any Machiavellian complexity. The same is true of the other famous dramatic moments in his life—his parading with the Pennsylvania militia he commanded, his walking the streets of Paris in Quaker homespun and an American fur cap, his meeting and embracing Voltaire before the French Academy. One readily sees the rhetorical motive in all these actions; they are rather more obvious than devious. For Melville to find in Franklin the blended "apostolic serpent and dove," a "tanned Machiavelli in tents," and a "deep worldly wisdom and polished Italian tact, gleaming under an air of Arcadian unaffectedness,"[35] is for a talented romantic, frankly, to romanticize, and to give to Franklin's rather blunt public gestures a load of "labyrinth-minded" ulterior meanings which they probably do not deserve.

It is my ultimate impression that, despite whatever reputation Franklin may have as a man of many faces, shrewd and worldly wise, that sanity for which he is so notable and which gives his writing its distinctive character is most deeply a kind of simplicity or selfharmoniousness. I think that Franklin is satisfying to read for something of the same reason "Snowbound" and John Woolman's journal are (the common Quaker background is no mere coincidence): the world his writings summon up—even when it includes the intrigues of London and Paris—is to us a kind of lost paradise. Reading Franklin, we can believe that once upon a time plain good sense could win through, and there was a world worth the winning—even as we acknowledge, in our sophistication, that there must have been a catch to it somewhere. I imagine that, as inheritors of an imposing apparatus of self-consciousness and self-analysis, we will probably continue to read Franklin, and to doubt him, for the mysterious sanity he achieved in an age before the world grew a subconscious.

NOTES

1. *The Autobiography of Benjamin Franklin*, ed. Leonard W. Labaree et al. (New Haven and London: Yale University Press, 1964), p. 163. Subse-

quent references to the *Autobiography* are to this edition, cited in the text.

2. *The Papers of Benjamin Franklin,* ed. Leonard W. Labaree et al. (New Haven: Yale University Press, 1959–), IV, 469. This edition of Franklin's works is cited below as *Papers.*

3. *Papers,* XI, 187.

4. Quoted by Carl Van Doren, *Benjamin Franklin* (New York: Viking Press, 1938, p. 606.

5. Herman Melville, *Israel Potter: His Fifty Years of Exile,* ed. Raymond Weaver (New York: Albert and Charles Boni, 1924), p. 75.

6. D. H. Lawrence, *Studies in Classic American Literature* (New York: Viking Press, 1964), p. 14.

7. Gladys Meyer, *Free Trade in Ideas: Aspects of American Liberalism Illustrated in Franklin's Philadelphia Career* (Morningside Heights, N.Y.: King's Crown Press, 1941), p. 70.

8. Carl Becker, *Benjamin Franklin* (Ithaca, N.Y.: Cornell University Press, 1946), p. 35.

9. Van Doren, p. 101.

10. Robert Sayre, *The Examined Self: Benjamin Franklin, Henry Adams, Henry James* (Princeton, N.J.: Princeton University Press, 1964), p. 25.

11. Max Farrand, "Self-Portraiture: The Autobiography," in *Meet Dr. Franklin* (Philadelphia: Franklin Institute, 1943), p. 32.

12. Theodore Hornberger, *Benjamin Franklin,* University of Minnesota Pamphlets on American Writers, No. 19 (Minneapolis: University of Minnesota Press, 1962), p. 5.

13. J. H. Plumb, "Ravaged by Common Sense," *New York Review of Books,* 19 April 1973, p. 8.

14. William Hanna, *Benjamin Franklin and Pennsylvania Politics* (Stanford, Calif.: Stanford University Press, 1964), p. 27; see also Meyer, pp. 71–76.

15. Erving Goffman, *The Presentation of Self in Everyday Life* (New York: Doubleday Anchor, 1959), p. 70.

16. George Herbert Mead, *Mind, Self & Society from the Standpoint of a Social Behaviorist,* ed. Charles W. Morris (Chicago: University of Chicago Press, 1934), p. 154.

17. Mead, p. 163.

18. Kenneth Burke, *A Rhetoric of Motives* (New York: Prentice-Hall, 1950), p. xiii.

19. Hendrik M. Ruitenbeek, *The Individual and the Crowd* (New York: Thomas Nelson & Sons, 1964), p. 128.

20. William James. *The Varieties of Religious Experience: A Study in Human Nature* (1902; rpt. New York: New American Library, 1958), p. 141.

21. Erik Erikson, "The Problem of Ego Identity," in *Identity and Anxiety: Survival of the Person in Mass Society,* eds. Maurice R. Stein, Arthur J. Vidich and David Manning White (Glencoe, Ill.: Free Press, 1960), p. 60.

22. Herbert Fingarette, "The Ego and Mystic Selflessness," in *Identity and Anxiety,* p. 560. Subsequent references to this article are cited in the text.

23. *Papers,* III, 481.

24. *Papers,* XIII, 188.

25. *Papers,* VII, 14.

26. *Papers,* II, 21.

27. Aldous Huxley, *Tomorrow and Tomorrow and Tomorrow and Other Essays* (1952; rpt. New York: New American Library, 1964), p. 51.

28. *Papers*, IV, 481.

29. Evelyn Underhill, *Mysticism: A Study in the Nature and Development of Man's Spiritual Consciousness* (New York: Meridian, 1911), p. 300.

30. Plumb, p. 8.

31. Paul W. Conner, *Poor Richard's Politicks: Benjamin Franklin and His New American Order* (New York: Oxford University Press, 1965), p. 211.

32. Plumb, p. 8.

33. Charles Sanford, "An American's *Pilgrim's Progress*," *American Quarterly*, 6 (1954), 307.

34. Conner, p. 213.

35. Melville, p. 72.

William L. Hedges

🏵 From Franklin to Emerson

1. Perry Miller and Connections in American Literature

To reread Perry Miller's well-known essay "From Edwards to Emerson" is to enter a half-forgotten world in which reputations, connections, and meanings in American literature were more nebulous than they have become for many scholars and critics since 1940.[1] Miller was surprisingly defensive in regard to Emerson, doubtful in his own mind, quite clearly, of the lasting value of so blithe a sage in an era of depression and world war, and well aware of pragmatic America's limited tolerance for mysticism and pantheism. In his essay, however, he unearthed native "roots" for transcendentalism, and his ironic innuendo managed to suggest a contemporary relevance for Emerson which foreshadowed a somewhat strained significance that students seem increasingly to find in American literature generally or in what is taken to be the dominant literary tradition in America.

The hackneyed metaphor of roots and soil justified itself by being part of a snide reference to Van Wyck Brooks, who had obviously failed in Miller's eyes to account satisfactorily for the "particular blossom" of Emerson "in the flowering of New England." Later in his essay the author of *The New England Mind* grumbled that the popular volume by Brooks, which had appeared four years earlier, although ostensibly a search for a usable American past, was based on insufficient knowledge of Emerson's period and of "the nature of social change in general." It is true that Brooks had done little to dispel the prevalent notion that Emerson was basically an amalgam of Kant, Coleridge, Swedenborg, the *Bhagvad-gita* and other assorted foreign influences. Brooks's explanation of Emerson was probably, for Miller, too close to that of Emerson himself, which Miller described sarcastically as seeing in transcendentalism "one more expression of the benign gentleman who previously had spoken in the persons of Socrates and Zoroaster, Mohammed and Buddha, Shakespeare and St. Paul."[2] Going to William James as an authority on religious experience, Brooks had argued that Emerson's doctrine of self-reliance was simply the reiteration of a fundamental idea or attitude implicit in "all the periods of revival, the early Christian age and Luther's age, Rousseau's, Kant's and Goethe's."[3]

Although Emerson identified transcendental idealism with a sequence of antiauthoritarian moments in philosophy and religion reaching back as far as the Stoics, Miller largely scoffed at his antihistoricism: it was part or parcel of transcendentalism's alarming eclecticism, its tendency to lump things together indiscriminately, its declaring "all ideas to be one idea, all religions the same religion, all poets singers of the same music." For Perry Miller in 1940 in the wake of the Nazi *Blitzkreig* it was imperative to be able to distinguish between the slayer and the slain, whatever their ultimate merger in the Over-Soul. So too it was necessary to insist "that ideas are born in time and place, that they spring from specific environments, that they express the force of societies and classes, that they are generated by power relations."[4]

And yet ironically Miller's own accounting for Emerson is in one sense not very different from that of Emerson or Brooks. Fundamental for all three is the notion of a periodic revival of religious enthusiasm. The difference is that Miller locates Emerson within the framework of a recurrent New England impulse in the direction of mystical piety, whereas for Emerson and Brooks the framework is much more vast. The two views, however, might well be made to coexist.

The heart of "From Edwards to Emerson" is the outline which Miller offers of the intellectual history of New England from 1630 to 1830. It emphasizes the polarity in Puritan thought, its intense piety and spirituality on the one hand and its diligent attention to the practical world on the other. As he put it, "At the core of the theology there was an indestructible element which was mystical, and a feeling for the universe which was almost pantheistic; but there was also a social code demanding obedience to external law, a code to which good people voluntarily conformed and to which bad people should be made to conform." This contradiction produced or characterized the conflicts between the Antinomians and John Winthrop and John Cotton and between Ed-

wards and Charles Chauncy. In the nineteenth century Miller saw a
recurrence of the same tension in the opposition between Emerson and
the Unitarians. Passing over the terror in Edwards at the wrath of the
Omnipotent, Miller stressed the revivalist's sense of the world as "dynamic . . . , filled with the presence of God, quickened with divine life,
pervaded with joy and ecstasy."[5] Edwards thus became an incipient
transcendentalist, held in check only by the bonds of Calvinist theology.
Emerson, Miller noted, was fortunate enough to have had Chauncy and
Unitarianism liberate New England (or at least Boston and Cambridge)
before the mystical pantheistic urge made its presence felt in himself.

Thus was transcendentalism given native roots, and mysticism and
pantheism Americanized. I hope I have made the reader a bit uneasy
by my glib use of "mysticism" and "pantheism." I deliberately echo
Miller, who I think is also uneasy with these words but who seems
determined to make the reader swallow them as representing the essential Emerson. What is amazing about the essay is that Miller largely
rejects a traditional view of Emerson that could easily have been made
to mesh with his interpretation of Puritanism. The view goes back at least
as far as James Russell Lowell, who laid it out very obviously in his deft
caricature of Emerson in "A Fable for Critics." The personality was
polarized: "Plotinus-Montaigne," Lowell called him, or "Greek head on
right Yankee shoulders." Why did Miller not look at Emerson as himself
an embodiment of the tension between the two pronounced tendencies
in New England thought, especially in view of Emerson's own fascination with polarities, his sense of experience as oscillation?

The answer is that to concede that Emerson had much of the
shrewd Yankee in him would have meant weakening what Miller obviously saw as Emerson's strongest claim for sympathy in 1940. Although
he specifically disclaims any interest in having the higher metaphysics of
transcendentalism taken "seriously" by his own contemporaries, Miller
does stress Emerson's sense of transcendentalism as a reaction against
the evils of the "commercial times" of Jacksonian America—as well as
against Unitarianism.[6] In Miller's mind, perhaps more than in Emerson's,
the "commercial times" are intimately connected with the social and
political conservatism of the worldly-minded commonsensical Unitarians.
Miller's depression-sharpened liberalism makes itself clearly felt. Call
Emerson a "mystagogue," as Lowell did, if you like, Miller seems to say,
but first and last there has been a lot of mystagoguery in America and
it has something to do with the dominance in this culture of the State
Street mentality and the failures of industrial capitalism.

The trouble is that for many the sharp distinction between Emerson and Yankee industry, frugality, and finance has been hard to maintain. Lowell was quite specific: Emerson's "range" was from the "pole"

of "Olympus" to that of "the Exchange." Bliss Perry began his *Emerson Today* in 1931 by noting the "open parable in the very lines of his face. . . . Seen from one side, it was the face of a Yankee of the old school, shrewd, serious, practical; the sort of face that may still be observed in the quiet country churches of New England or at the village store. Seen from the other side, it was the face of a dreamer, a seer, a soul brooding on things to come, things as yet very far away."[7] While Miller in the lead article of the December 1940 issue of *The New England Quarterly* was relating transcendental pantheism to puritan piety, Alexander C. Kern in "Emerson and Economics," the final article, was suggesting that the "influence of Emerson's puritan New England background" on the "crass portion of his thought" was much stronger than had generally been noticed. Emphasizing the conflict in Emerson between materialism and idealism, Kern argued the fundamental domination of the latter but admitted that the Emersonian concern with practical endeavor sometimes amounted to almost overt advocacy of "rugged individualism."[8] The next year Miller's colleague F. O. Matthiessen was to suggest that Emerson's "most balanced" assessment of his own position "was that which placed him between the transcendentalists and Franklin."[9] And Miller himself was later in speaking of Emerson to praise his "levelheadedness" as "his most precious bequest to a posterity which is understandably exasperated by his unction."[10]

Miller would have been the first to recognize that his own thought, as much as Emerson's, was a product of a particular time and place. It is well, however, for those of us who utilize his ideas to develop an equal awareness. I propose therefore an inquiry into Emerson's relation to Benjamin Franklin to balance Miller's study of Emerson and Edwards. My primary purposes concern the two classic American sages themselves: if, as I believe, they are closer to each other than Miller would have admitted, then we are missing something important in both of them if we ignore the affinity.

True, nothing is more commonplace in Emerson scholarship than recognition of the tension between his practicality and his piety.[11] But "From Edwards to Emerson" has given comfort to those who would rather forget Emerson's pragmatic side. These days Emerson's detractors— of whom there are still a fair number, especially among devotees of Thoreau, Hawthorne, and Melville—are apt to be the ones who make the most of his interest in wealth, power, and success. It is not uncommon to find him at least briefly compared to Franklin, but the Franklin who is invoked in the most detailed and extended comparison that I know of is a one-dimensional figure, a flat abstraction out of Max Weber.[12]

In the back of my mind also is a sense that Miller's widely reprinted essay serves as keystone in an overarching framework of general concepts which for many people greatly affect the ways in which American literature is seen and interpreted.[13] What, one wonders, is the strength of the whole structure if the keystone is loose or out of line? This is a question I propose only to raise, not answer, except to say generally that I believe there is cause for concern. But let me, before getting on with Franklin and Emerson, briefly explain what I take to be the larger significance of "From Edwards to Emerson."

These days Emerson is much less apologized for than he was in 1940. If Thoreau seems to many to have given a more thoroughly satisfying literary expression to basic Emersonian insights and awareness than the master himself, the seminal power of Emerson in the development of a central tradition in American literature is now not only recognized but much more fully understood. The year after Miller's essay Matthiessen in *American Renaissance* demonstrated the fundamental modernity of the sensibility of Emerson and his illustrious contemporaries Thoreau, Hawthorne, Melville, and Whitman. And once the significance of Emerson's theory of language and poetics was more clearly discerned, the temptation to dismiss transcendentalism as moonshine diminished. Matthiessen paid less attention to the early native roots of the American renaissance than to its affinities with some of the baroque and metaphysical literature which the taste of T. S. Eliot and other moderns had resuscitated. But the net effect was very much the same, especially after Edward Taylor became better known and after Edwards's *Images or Shadows of Divine Things* was published by Miller and the Puritan interest in symbolism came to be more and more fully explored.

Something like what Miller called Puritan "piety, a religious passion, the sense of an inward communication and of the divine symbolism of nature" came to seem the motive being realized most powerfully in a great deal of American literature.[14] Indeed it may not be too much to say that there gradually emerged out of the conjunction of implications in the works of the two Harvard professors—one focusing primarily on the seventeenth and the other on the nineteenth centuries—a theory or ideology of American literature which has won wide acceptance. It is a theory which sees the main tradition leaping from early Puritanism into the mid-nineteenth century and which tends to ignore much that came between. Miller made the vital connection between Puritan piety and transcendentalism with an enthusiasm and a flair for irony which have a lot to do with his essay's continuing appeal. What he suggests is what has been said over and over again since 1940 in discussions of major tendencies and developments in American literature: in essence that literature is not what we should expect it to be. It is not primarily a body of open straightforward, realistic, practical-minded, commonsensical expression, the embodiment of progressive dreams, but rather something private, cryptic, symbolic, mysterious, sometimes mystic, often night-marishly fantastic. Obviously the irony implicit in what I am calling the ideology of American literature is congenial to the modern (and post-modern) sensibility and its dionysian distrust of the pragmatic and the merely rational. An inquiry into Franklin and Emerson therefore is to some extent an exercise in distrust of that distrust.

2. FRANKLIN TO EMERSON

We may begin by noting that in 1962 Miller published an essay on Edwards and Franklin. Perhaps had he lived longer he would himself have completed what I hope to make clear ought to be seen as a natural or logical triangulation. As was to be expected, he found in Franklin the perfect foil for Edwards that so many others have seen and, in the con-trast between the two "massively symbolic characters," a made-to-order representation of the split in Puritanism which he had posted two decades earlier. That the split still lived on in the mid-twentieth century he im-plicitly demonstrated by showing his own admiration for Edwardsean piety coupling snugly with an inherent skepticism and irreverence. He responded with gusto to Franklin's independent-mindedness, his shrewd wit, his down-to-earth style and his ribaldry. He saw an understanding of Franklin as an important part of an understanding of America. And finally he saw a crucial connection: underneath the surface Edwards was "Franklin's brother."[15]

Why? Because of what Carl Becker had called Franklin's "disin-terestedness." Miller observed that in the "most perceptive sentence yet written about Franklin," Becker had said "that it was no wonder he sought for his ultimate satisfaction in natural science, because only in the physical universe could he find a 'disinterestedness' equal to his own." Going on, Miller wrote that "one learns to appreciate that the actual charm of [Franklin's] writing is his disengagement from all the multi-farious activities of his career. He could never have . . . written about them . . . in exactly the quizzical spirit he unfailingly maintains, unless he had somewhere in his intricate constitution an ultimate sense that all . . . local aims were subordinate to a larger one, in relation to which they were indeed trivial." In the end Miller sensed that Franklin the "master worldly-wiseman," like Edwards the "archspiritualist," somehow felt himself a "negligible finite in the face of a glorious incomprehensi-bility."[16] Thus piety and practicality merge.

Emerson, I shall maintain, felt and responded to this same quality in Franklin which Becker and Miller tried to define as disinterestedness or disengagement. The terminology may not be quite adequate to the elusiveness of the attitude in question. Were it not for the fact that no one shows less indication of having gone through a dark night of the soul than Franklin, Eliot's prayer from "Ash-Wednesday," "Teach us to care and not to care," might serve as appropriate text for the peculiar equilibrium one senses in Franklin. But let us put it this way, that Franklin's empiricism was something more than a commitment to scientific method; it was a receptivity to experience and its complex possibilities that *practically* speaking amounted to reverence—or to what Emerson might have called absolute trust, the self-reliance that is ultimately reliance on Nature. One thinks of the third paragraph of "Self-Reliance," with its paradoxical movement from the "iron-string" of "Trust thyself" to what seems a contradictory imperative, "Accept the place the divine providence has found for you, the society of your contemporaries, the connection of events. Great men have always done so, and confided themselves childlike to the genius of their age, betraying their perception that the absolutely trustworthy was seated at their heart, working through their hands, predominating in all their being." We shall be reminded of this reference to heart and hands a bit later.

To the author of "Self-Reliance," Franklin was quite clearly a great man. His name appears frequently on the lists of great men which Emerson compiled in his notebooks and journals.[17] And part of the greatness obviously was his capacity for feeling perfectly at home in the world. Emerson comments explicitly on the "extraordinary ease" with which Franklin's mind worked; he was "unconscious of any mental effort in detailing the profoundest solutions of phenomena & therefore [made] no parade" (*Journals*, II, 208). And in 1841 he wrote, "When the great man comes, he will have that social strength which Dr. Kirkland or Dr. Franklin or Robert Burns had & so will engage us to the moment that we shall not suspect his greatness until late afterward[;] in some dull hour we shall say I am enlarged. . . . This man! this man! whence came he?" (*Journals*, VIII, 126–27).

Franklin's early "Articles of Belief and Acts of Religion" are a clear indication of the coexistence in him of impulses that, for all their connection with the early Enlightenment, suggest Edwards and traditional Puritanism on the one hand and on the other Emerson and transcendentalism. He acknowledges himself as "less than nothing" in the face of the supreme perfection of the "INFINITE." And yet he conceives human happiness and pleasure to be part of the system created by that Infinite Being, who in Himself can have no regard for man. As elsewhere in Franklin, virtue and happiness are conceived of as bound together, though the logic of the relationship is quite unclear. Superficially this may seem to point toward the total secularization and hence vulgarization of the Protestant ethic and the notion that material success is demonstration of moral virtue. Or he may seem simply shallow in equating virtue with happiness rather than suffering. There certainly is a material dimension to the pleasure which this religious confession is so much concerned with: it involves awareness of a world in which "many Things . . . seem purely design'd for the Delight of Man"—though this emphasis, it is worth observing, represents a welcome awakening out of Puritan inhibition. But one suspects a kernel of deep awareness in the assertion that "without Virtue Man can have no Happiness in this World."[18]

The absoluteness of the statement is what startles: "*no* happiness" except with virtue. This goes farther than routine neoclassical couplings of happiness and virtue such as the one in the excerpt from Addison's *Cato* which Franklin uses as an inscription to the "Articles of Belief." It suggests the surprising intensity of his personification of virtue a few weeks later in the third of the "Busy-Body" papers—the idealized figure of an American "Cato," a compound of "Innocence and Wisdom" dressed in "plainest Country Garb," whose moral force, apparent in "the Air of his Face" and "every Part of his Behavior," compels "Respect from every Person in the Room." And one thinks ahead also from "without Virtue . . . no Happiness" to Emerson's "All things are moral" and Thoreau's pronouncement from the tranquility of *Walden,* "Our whole life is startlingly moral. There is never an instant's truce between virtue and vice. Goodness is the only investment that never fails."[19] Franklin is obviously active rather than meditative, more interested in *doing* good than in contemplating the nature of goodness. And yet when he talks of the "inward Joy" of "ADORATION," one wonders for an instant who was the incipient transcendentalist, he or Edwards.[20] In any case his "Articles of Belief" represent the man of reason in effect throwing up his hands, confiding himself to the genius of the world, which is ultimately irrational or incomprehensible. This is the larger context of his empiricism.

In some passages Emerson sees Franklin as we would expect a transcendentalist to see him. In the lecture on Milton we hear, "Franklin's man is a frugal, inoffensive, thrifty citizen, but savours of nothing heroic." On another occasion he associates Franklin with the "vulgar Utilitarianism" of the late eighteenth century, content with "Common Sense" and incapable of transcendental "Reason."[21] But on the whole Emerson's response to Franklin is surprisingly positive. While most of his references to him in the journals occur in the 1820s and 1830s—and we may speculate that Franklin came to mean less to him in his later years—the frugal man of common sense also figured earlier as a "moral philosopher" and revolutionary (*Journals,* II, 208) and was clearly involved in the original formulation of some key Emersonian ideas.

To begin with, the American Revolution was a crucial event in Emerson's sense of his heritage. It marked for him an epoch of mental and moral as well as political liberation. In the same entry in which he marveled at Franklin's intellectual brilliance, he declared, "That age abounded in greatness," and he compared it with his own, in which "men . . . do not produce new works but admire old ones" (II, 208). In another early entry he wrote of "the cowed benevolence of" his own "dismal time" (*Journals*, IV, 37). His dim view of the present, so crucial to *Nature*, "Self-Reliance," and especially "The American Scholar," clearly formed itself against a strong sense of the preceding age as nonretrospective. "Where is the master that could have instructed Franklin or Washington," he wrote in 1832, going on to add, "or Bacon or Newton?" (*Journals*, IV, 50). He reiterated the question in "Self-Reliance." He also transcribed in his journal the Latin inscription (by Turgot) from Houdon's bust of Franklin, which in English reads, "He snatched the thunderbolt from heaven, then the scepter from tyrants" (*Journals*, VI, 208).

At the same time, one sees that Emerson's conception of the Revolutionary period is intimately tied to his sense of himself as a New Englander. It is not Jefferson or Patrick Henry he looks back to, but James Otis, John Hancock, Samuel Adams, and in that context Franklin, born only a few doors away from the Emerson house in Boston. And the Revolutionary group relate to Bradford, Winthrop, Mather, and Edwards. If there is any division in this heritage for Emerson, it is between the overzealousness of the seventeenth-century Puritans and the comparative moderation of their eighteenth-century descendants—a view, by the way, which Otis and Sam Adams make difficult to substantiate. The earlier period had seen lamentable excesses of bigotry and persecution; it was well that the original Puritan ardor had cooled down into the "*Good Sense*" which he at first thought Franklin, but then realized Gibbon, had called "as rare as genius." All in all Emerson valued his "Puritan stock" for its "vigorous sense, or practical genius" (*Journals*, II, 197, 227). Its piety he seems to have taken for granted. He was at one point, very early, disturbed by Franklin's reputation for skepticism, but before long let himself be persuaded—rather too easily, one is tempted to conclude— that the philosopher who stole the thunderbolt from heaven believed in immortality (*Journals*, II, 108, 208).

Franklin, it may be argued, was for Emerson a model of the American scholar. His life obviously taught the greater importance of "observation of men & things" over books as a source of knowledge. He and, intriguingly, Edwards were the early American writers who Emerson thought showed most clearly the stamp of a native American genius (*Journals*, II, 230, 197). As one would expect, he clearly admired Franklin's delight in proverbial wisdom. In Franklin's style, one suspects, Emerson felt himself in touch with one thing he was looking for in poetry

—"the common": the "meal in the firkin; the milk in the pan; the ballad in the street; the news of the boat."²² In a journal passage which must offend those who see Franklin primarily as the embodiment of smugness, Emerson observed that the "greatest men have been most thoughtful for the humblest. Socrates, . . . Alfred, Franklin, Jesus Christ, & all the Pauls and Fenelons he has made. . . . And, so keep me, heaven, I will love the race in general if I cannot in any particular" (*Journals*, IV, 315). So Emerson apparently was not one of the readers put off by the addition of "Humility," with its attendant exhortation, "Imitate Jesus and Socrates," to Franklin's list of virtues.²³

At times in talking about Franklin, Emerson balances him against an opposing tendency in a polar relationship, thus seeming to sever practical ingenuity completely from morality or spirituality. "Transcendentalism says, the Man is all," he observes, whereas "Franklin says, the tools. . . ." And in another passage he substitutes for the conventional head/heart dichotomy one between hand and heart, "the hand of Franklin & the heart of Paul." Yet even as he makes the distinctions there is a sense of an ultimate relationship, as is implied in the passage from "Self-Reliance" quoted above that "the absolutely trustworthy" being "seated" at the "heart" and working through the "hands." Both Franklin and Paul are examples of trust in oneself, secure "among gluttons & sycophants." And, "A master *and* tools,—is the lesson I read in every shop and farm and library" (*Journals*, III, 249; X, 53–54).

What Franklin represents for Emerson is the practical side of Puritanism, which for the most part he found it impossible to repudiate, however much he may have wanted to, because Nature is real as well as ideal, fact as well as spirit. The soul, at least in this life, is nothing without the body. The body has to be cared for, and taking care of the body or learning to cope with the physical demands of Nature is the beginning of the cultivation of the mind or spirit. Franklin, the journals suggest, belongs as much with the "Discipline" chapter of *Nature* as with "Commodity." As early as 1830 Emerson associates him with the phrase "the conduct of life" and calls him one of the "astonishing instances" of it. And the very next entry in the journal deals with the subject of virtue in a way strongly reminiscent of Franklin (*Journals*, III, 200).²⁴

First comes an insistence on virtue as action, *doing* good, not just talking about it. The problem, as in Franklin, is method, how to produce virtue. And the answer is surprisingly similar to Franklin's. It is asounding to discover that Emerson may have taken seriously just that part of Franklin which most tempts the modern reader's laughter or derision, that "bold and arduous Project of arriving at moral Perfection."²⁵ Instead of talking about all the virtues being "comprehended" in "self-trust" he specifies individual virtues that are worth acquiring, starting with "Early

Spartan rising," then "Temperance" and "fasting," after which he calls for "attention to . . . personal habits."[26] The habits that Emerson is most concerned to cultivate tend, it is true, to reveal his predilection for contemplation over action. If he has Franklin's list of virtues in mind, he seems to get stalled on "Silence," as he notes the value of the "habit of being sometimes alone, the habit of reading, the habit of abstraction in order to find out what his own opinion is, the habit of controlling his conversation, the habit of praying, or referring himself always to God." For Emerson, of course, piety ultimately transcends practicality. But the respect for a discipline which recognizes the close relationship of body and mind, appetite and morality, remains somewhat Franklinesque. He ends the passage with a sentence which sounds like something Franklin might have written had he tried to get transcendental resonances into Poor Richard's maxims: "Order has a good name in the world for getting the most sweetness out of time" (*Journals*, III, 200).

Thirty years later the phrase "the conduct of life" surfaced as the title of a book by Emerson in which the essay "Wealth" holds a position somewhat comparable to that of "Discipline" in *Nature*. Or, more accurately, "Wealth" is like an expanded merger of "Commodity" and "Discipline." It is crucial because it makes clear that the Emersonian ethic was the Protestant ethic in a highly exalted form, an effort, like the one implicit in Franklin's life and writings, to fuse piety and practicality, to maintain that work, virtue, salvation, and enjoyment of the world are functions of one another.[27] As the first two paragraphs quickly demonstrate, "Wealth" is an elaboration of the basic Puritan idea of the calling:

> As soon as a stranger is introduced . . . , one of the first questions which all wish to have answered is, How does that man get his living? And with reason. He is no whole man until he knows how to earn a blameless livelihood. Society is barbarous until every industrious man can get his living without dishonest customs.
>
> Every man is a consumer, and ought to be a producer. He fails to make his place good in the world unless he not only pays his debt but also adds something to the common wealth. Nor can he do justice to his genius without making some larger demand on the world than a bare subsistence. He is by constitution expensive, and needs to be rich.

Already Emerson's conception of the calling has become exorbitant and implies an openness to enjoyment which, like Franklin's, we do not ordinarily associate with Puritanism. With an expansiveness that suggests Whitman, he is soon saying that man "is born to be rich. He . . . is tempted out by his appetites and fancies to the conquest of this and that piece of nature, until he finds his well-being in the use of his planet, and of more planets than his own. . . . The same correspondence that is between thirst in the stomach and water in the spring, exists between the whole of man and the whole of nature." But the connection between wealth and virtue or discipline is never laid by. "The subject of economy mixes itself with morals, inasmuch as it is a peremptory point of virtue that a man's independence be secured. Poverty demoralizes."

To find the way to wealth—what Emerson would consider "true" wealth—is to acquire transcendental discipline. Character is formed by honest labor in a calling, since "wealth is in applications of mind to nature" and respect for the laws of nature. It necessitates the formulation of rules, the creation of "a better order." Emerson's observation in "Wealth" that the "counting-room maxims liberally expounded are laws of the universe" is an updating of his famous Aunt Mary's declaration, "I respect in a rich man the order of Providence."[28] In sum Emerson sees a legitimate pursuit of wealth as consistent with the natural order, part of Nature's functioning to fully humanize man. The concept of economy ultimately involves the satisfaction of moral and spiritual as well as material wants. Dishonest gain is thus not true wealth. To the charge that dishonesty pays, Emerson would reply, it is an illusion; in the long run fraud produces material and moral waste, which touches everyone.

Emerson is close here to a central perception in Franklin, which develops with his realization that he could dispense with revelation as far as morality is concerned. Both men assume an ultimate connection between self-interest and cosmic well-being. Franklin's secularization of morality begins with his daring to think, as he tells us in the *Autobiography,* that "vicious Actions are not hurtful because they are forbidden, but forbidden because they are hurtful, the Nature of Man alone consider'd." Applied only to success in business, his belief that "*Truth, Sincerity and Integrity* in Dealings between Man and Man" are "good" for one may seem naive. But when that belief expands suddenly to the far-reaching hypothesis that, "all the Circumstances of things considered," moral actions are beneficial to one, he brings us to the wisdom of a world in which if everyone behaved decently to one another, everyone would prosper.[29]

3. FRANKLIN AND EMERSON: THE NAME OF THE GAME

What tries the patience of the twentieth-century mind is the way in which Emerson and Franklin sometimes seem to take the connection between wealth and virtue too much for granted or interpret "wealth" too literally. We are skeptical when Franklin says that "no Qualities" are "so likely to make a poor Man's Fortune as those of Probity and Integrity."[30] *The Great Gatsby* is more real to us than *Poor Richard.* The pursuit of success demoralizes—as much as poverty: that is our fear. Commercialism distracts attention from the higher values in Emerson's economics and virtually guarantees waste and exploitation. Emerson's daring is apt to startle us more than he intended when in "Wealth" he says, "I have never seen a rich man. I have never seen a man as rich as all men ought to be." For metaphor most of us would probably prefer Thoreau's curiously parallel observation, "I have never yet met a man who was quite awake. How could I have looked him in the face?"[31] Disinterestedness has its limitations, its proximity, through indifference, to callousness.

While Franklin and Emerson are polar figures, each is polarized within himself between the attractions of practicality and contemplation. There is a certain remoteness or splendid isolation—some call it complacency—in both, Franklin's gregariousness notwithstanding. He is much more involved in the day-to-day world than Emerson, but, as Miller and Becker maintained, not completely so. There is a casualness about him that sometimes disappoints us. Promising as the *Autobiography* is, for instance, as a record of self-education and self-liberation in a society moving toward self-government, he shows no signs of wanting to push his awareness, particularly his self-awareness, any further than circumstances seem to require. There is a point in the consideration of moral issues beyond which he apparently does not want to get involved, perhaps on the assumption that in the long run the practical differences are negligible. Openmindedness, his greatest virtue, comes to seem at times an evasion of the responsibility of being serious down to the deepest level. Thus his mistakes remain mere "errata," typographical errors in the little book of his life.

The happy side of this failing, if such it should be called, is that he is a less somber, less pompous wise man, seer, or lay preacher than he is often taken to be—which is to acknowledge the depth of his sense of humor, its inextricable tie with his wisdom. The complex and subtle Franklin who emerges from recent scholarship and criticism has more in common with Emerson than did Franklin the plain-style Puritan or no-nonsense apostle of reason and utility.[32] We see his irony looking askance at his own moralizing out of a wry awareness of human (including his own) limitations lodged within a broad vision of human possibility. He preached as much as any Puritan, but no one was more aware than he that he was not better than he should be—as he shows at the beginning of the *Autobiography* by the pains he takes to call attention to his vanity: he is writing basically to please himself. When we see him in effect thanking God for his vanity "with all humility," we begin to see the man in his humor.[33]

Like Emerson, he is sententious in both the good and bad senses. Both lay down rules of conduct in aphoristic rather than legalistic language, aiming not so much for precision as for provocation, to startle the reader or listener into sudden awareness. Franklin's interest in rules, law, and order was perhaps fundamentally, though he scarcely realized it himself, a function of an aesthetic awareness, of his recognition that the way something is said determines what is said, that admonition or prohibition, effectively conceived or formulated, is liberating, not restrictive, illuminating, not stupefying.

A sage with a high sense of drama, he may be as much artist as scientist. It is true that as a man of affairs he generally took a practical view of the arts, in theory writing to inform, instruct, and persuade, putting a high premium on the most directly communicative qualities in style. *"Heavenly Father,"* he argues, "is more concise, equally expressive, and better modern English" than *"Our Father which art in Heaven."*[34] His devastating criticism of a song by Handel[35] puts so much stress on the words coming through clearly that one may wonder what, if anything, he heard in the music, whether he conceived of artistic expression as anything more than the direct transference from one brain to another of a few simple ideas—the utilitarian aesthetic, essentially, of the *Bay Psalm Book*. Yet obviously Franklin did not always mean business when he wrote. One finds him too often taking a delight in forms and formality that quite belies the virtual philistinism of his insistence on the purely didactic function of literature.

Consider, for instance, the artfulness with which he contrives a letter of condolence:

> We have lost a most dear and valuable relation, but it is the will of
> God and Nature that these mortal bodies be laid aside, when the
> soul is to enter into real life; 'tis rather an embrio state, a preparation
> for living; a man is not completely born until he be dead: Why then
> should we grieve that a new child is born among the immortals?
> A new member added to their happy society?

One may doubt the strength of Franklin's faith in death as a new birth, but something in him rises to the occasion. Having decided to use a conventional form of commiseration, he works the whole letter out with neat precision. The elegance of his final image of death—an invitation to an eternal "party of pleasure"—has the authentic ring of something he would have liked to believe.[36]

He uses standard flourishes like the letter of condolence or congratulations to help him define himself in various social roles, personalizing the gestures, of course, often giving new life to shopworn sentiments. On happy occasions, he sometimes mocks rituals that threaten to turn into empty formalities. Standard forms and models, neoclassic formality, rather than a sense of organic form, moved him. Yet he could tell when a form did not fit a subject and could play on the discovery, often making

fun of himself in the process. Gallantry was his forte, especially with
women much younger than himself in whom his interest was supposed to
be more or less paternal. In response to a letter received during a winter
storm he writes, "Your Favours come mixd with the Snowy Fleeces which
are pure as your Virgin Innocence, white as your lovely Bosom, and—as
cold:—But let it warm toward some worthy young Man."[37] Another time
the "fatherly Advice" he offers this lady becomes not only slightly risqué
self-mockery, but also a parody of the advice-giving routine on which
The Way to Wealth was later to be based. "Be a good Girl," he writes.

> Go constantly to Meeting . . . till you get a good Husband. . . . You
> must practise *Addition* to your Husband's Estate, by Industry and
> Frugality; *Substraction* of all unnecessary Expenses; *Multiplication*
> (I would gladly have taught you that myself, but you thought it
> was time enough, and wou'dn't learn) he will soon make you a
> Mistress of it. As to *Division*, I say with Brother Paul, *Let there be
> no Divisions among ye.*[38]

For Franklin the conduct of life, as commentators are fond of
noting, seems to have involved his self-dramatization in appropriate roles
as much as it did the daily discipline of forming steady habits. We may
see "cosmetic" image-making in his acting out the diligent tradesman for
all Philadelphia to see or his playing the homespun American in Paris.
Perhaps Emerson would have scented hypocrisy or self-deception in his
shifting roles, or at any rate interpreted concessions to public opinion as
inconsistent with a self-reliant nonconformity. But Emerson's conception
of self-reliance was not withdrawal into a narrow privacy. He knew
about complicated selves from personal experience. Given his sense of
the self as so much of the time shifting, oscillating in a world of illusion,
self-reliance becomes for him something more than a routine discipline.
The Franklin who self-consciously plays social roles, who "loves," as
Benjamin DeMott says, "to stage virtues,"[39] and who as a writer speaks
through numerous personae seems ultimately a compatriot in cunning
of the philosopher who in "Self-Reliance" warns against a "foolish consistency," who in the same essay admits his willingness, if need be, to
speak from the devil and who alternately identifies with representative
men of such radically different persuasions as Montaigne and Swedenborg, the democrat and the aristocrat, the slayer and the slain.

From the immediate or existential point of view both Emerson and
Franklin see chaos in experience almost as often as order and harmony.
In theory, however, they regard the world from another viewpoint as
well—from the aspect of eternity. And the two views blending together at
times transform confusion into mystery and surprise. The world becomes
an infinitely intricate and entrancing work of art. Or to shift to, and at

the same time recast, Carl Becker's image of Franklin looking at public affairs as a game,[40] life in general becomes for both of these shrewd observers a game, in which the object is to discover the rules—and they are infinitely complex. It is a game in which one does the best one can on proverbial wisdom and fresh observations of nature—a parcel of partial, relative insights—and with some part of the mind enjoys watching oneself play, surprised by the tricks life plays and excited by sudden discoveries and occasional tricks of one's own. In this game fair play and trickery are assumed to be ultimately compatible.

Trial-and-error is the name of the game. Both Emerson and Franklin are empiricists, trying to learn from an experience which has its endless complications. In the *Autobiography* Franklin observes himself making his picaresque way through life, sometimes in control of himself and the situation, sometimes simply running in luck, sometimes being victimized or remaining largely passive—though willing—lacking a sure sense of direction, having to respond to events he has scarcely anticipated. And this life, even with all its spectacular success, has more than a little in common with the experience which Emerson analyzes in terms of fate, polarities, and illusions.

Given the nature of this experience, both men take refuge in cosmic optimism. The serenity or tranquility of Franklin seems more actual, Emerson's more theoretical. In both, however, there is an oft-commented-on coldness. Too much has probably been made of it in both cases, yet the coldness still seems an important link between the two. For if, as Miller maintains, Franklin's "boredom with humanity" is what makes him Jonathan Edwards' brother,[41] then it must make him Emerson's great-uncle as well. And Yankee reticence will perhaps come to be seen as an indication that the split in Puritanism divides the individual within himself as much as it divides man from man. While the outward eye is alert to the practical, the would-be "transparent eyeball" of the inner self, alone with what circulates as "currents of the Universal Being,"[42] winks. On the verge of becoming nothing while seeing everything, the Yankee knows enough to smile—as Becker sensed Franklin smiling at the signing of the Declaration of Independence—and hold his peace.[43]

NOTES

1. The essay, originally called "Johnathan Edwards to Emerson," was first published in *New England Quarterly*, 13 (1940), 589–617. Miller reprinted it under the title "From Edwards to Emerson" in *Errand into the Wilderness* (Cambridge: Harvard University Press, 1956), the version cited in this essay.

2. *Errand into the Wilderness*, pp. 187, 200, 188.

3. Van Wyck Brooks, *The Flowering of New England 1815–1865* (n.p.: Dutton, 1936), p. 207.

4. *Errand into the Wilderness*, p. 187.

5. *Ibid.*, pp. 192, 195.

6. Ibid., pp. 186–87, 188. The phrase "commercial times" Miller takes from Emerson, *Works* (Boston, 1904), I, 339.

7. Bliss Perry, *Emerson Today* (Princeton: Princeton University Press), p. 1.

8. Alexander C. Kern, "Emerson and Economics," *New England Quarterly*, 13 (1940), 683, 681.

9. F. O. Matthiessen, *American Renaissance* (New York: Oxford University Press, 1941), p. 66.

10. Perry Miller, "Emersonian Genius and the American Democracy," *New England Quarterly*, 26 (1953), 43.

11. In his *Emerson Handbook* (New York: Hendricks House, 1953) Frederic Ives Carpenter lists *"The Two Sides of the Face"* as the first major problem in Emerson biography and maintains, "There are not only two sides to Emerson's face and philosophy, but also two (or more) interpretations of each side. The best biographies are those which recognize and describe this dualism without falsely simplifying its complexity" (pp. 1, 3).

12. See Jesse Bier, "Weberism, Franklin, and the Transcendental Style," *New England Quarterly*, 43 (1970), 179–92. Contrasting Emerson unfavorably with Thoreau, Bier reads the opposition of piety and practicality in the older transcendentalist as hypocrisy, self-deception, or confusion. Interestingly he ridicules Kern for having put a more favorable construction on Emerson's "ambivalence," charging him with having written a "simple apologia" (p. 191).

13. I have made no systematic investigation of the reprinting of "From Edwards to Emerson," but its popularity in books of essays designed to supplement college and university courses in American literature is obvious. It is included in *Interpretations of American Literature*, ed. Charles Feidelson and and Paul Brodtkorb (New York: Oxford University Press, 1959); *American Literature: A Critical Survey*, ed. T. D. Young and R. E. Fine (New York: American Book Co., 1968); and *Theories of American Literature*, ed. D. M. Kartiganer and M. A. Griffith (New York: Macmillan, 1972).

14. *Errand into the Wilderness*, p. 192.

15. Miller, "Benjamin Franklin, 1706–1790, Jonathan Edwards, 1703–1758," in *Major Writers of America*, gen. ed. Perry Miller (New York: Harcourt, Brace & World, 1962), I, 97, 95.

16. Ibid., I, 95, 96.

17. *The Journals and Miscellaneous Notebooks of Ralph Waldo Emerson*, ed. William H. Gilman et al. (Cambridge: Harvard University Press, 1960–), I, 193, 250; II, 227; III, 200, 357; IV, 36, 50, 315. (This work is subsequently referred to by volume and page numbers in parentheses in the text.) Franklin's greatness was the subject of a draft of an early composition in the *Journals* (II, 223–24).

18. *The Papers of Benjamin Franklin*, ed. Leonard W. Labaree et al. (New Haven: Yale University Press, 1959–), I, 102–3.

19. For the "Busy-Body," see *Papers*, I, 119. Emerson's statement occurs in the "Discipline" chapter of *Nature*, which speaks of the "ethical character" penetrating "the bone and marrow of nature." Thoreau's statement is from "Higher Laws" in *Walden*.

20. *Papers*, I, 104.

21. *The Early Lectures of Ralph Waldo Emerson*, ed. Stephen E. Whicher et al. (Cambridge: Harvard University Press, 1959, 1964) I, 150; II, 67. Even so, in the latter passage Franklin remains for Emerson "the clearest name" of

his period, in contrast to "Rousseau and Voltaire, Diderot and other unclean democrats." For other less flattering references to Franklin, *see Journals*, V, 202; VI, 232; VIII, 398.

22. Emerson, "The American Scholar." He makes note of aphorisms, epigrams, and fables by Franklin in *Journals*, II, 208, 237, 377; IV, 132; VI, 170.

23. *The Autobiography of Benjamin Franklin*, ed. Leonard W. Labaree et al. (New Haven: Yale University Press, 1964), p. 150. Emerson elsewhere links Franklin and Socrates for their humility (*Journals*, X, 298) and also speaks of the latter's "Franklin-like wisdom" ("Plato; or, The Philosopher" in *Representative Men*; cf. *Journals*, X, 482).

24. The two entries were made three weeks apart but are closely enough linked in subject matter to suggest that Emerson probably reread the first just before or while writing the second.

25. *Autobiography*, p. 148.

26. As in "The American Scholar."

27. Kern suggests the connection between Emerson and the Protestant ethic in *New England Quarterly*, 13 (1940), 683.

28. Quoted by Miller, *Errand into the Wilderness*, p. 201.

29. *Autobiography*, pp. 114–15, 158.

30. *Autobiography*, p. 158.

31. Henry David Thoreau, *Walden* ("Where I Lived, and What I Lived For").

32. J. A. Leo Lemay's "Franklin and the *Autobiography*: An Essay on Recent Scholarship," *Eighteenth-Century Studies*, 1 (1967–68), 185–211, gives some sense of the emerging Franklin. The essay calls particular attention to Franklin's virtues as a humorist (p. 195). In a more recent article, "Benjamin Franklin," in *Major Writers of Early American Literature*, ed. Everett Emerson (Madison: University of Wisconsin Press, 1972), pp. 205–43, Lemay depicts a writer of great artfulness and subtlety, thoroughly accustomed to directing and controlling the attitudes and emotions of his readers through sophisticated fictional contrivances which frequently obscure or mask his real identity or motive. Other recent works which stress the contradictions and complexities of Franklin and his writings are John W. Ward, "Who Was Benjamin Franklin?" *American Scholar*, 32 (1963), 541–53; David Levin, "*The Autobiography of Benjamin Franklin:* The Puritan Experimenter in Life and Art," *Yale Review*, 53 (1963), 258–75; Robert F. Sayre, *The Examined Self: Benjamin Franklin, Henry Adams, Henry James* (Princeton: Princeton University Press, 1964).

33. *Autobiography*, pp. 44–45.

34. *Benjamin Franklin: Representative Selections, with Introduction, Bibliography, and Notes*, ed. Frank L. Mott and Chester E. Jorgenson (New York: American Book Co., 1936), p. 415.

35. Ibid., pp. 351–54.

36. *Papers*, VI, 406–7.

37. *Papers*, V, 503.

38. *Papers*, VI, 225.

39. Benjamin DeMott, *New York Times Book Review*, 5 July 1964, p. 19.

40. Carl Becker, in *Dictionary of American Biography*, VI (1931), 597.

41. Perry Miller, "Benjamin Franklin, 1706–1790, Jonathan Edwards, 1703–58," I, 97.

42. Emerson, *Nature* ("Nature").

43. Becker, *D. A. B.*

🐚 Contributors

PERCY G. ADAMS, Director of Graduate Studies in English at the University of Tennessee, is author of *Travelers and Travel Liars: 1660–1800*, translator and editor of *Crèvecoeur's Eighteenth-Century Travels in Pennsylvania and New York*, General Editor of Dover Publications' series of Great Travel Books of the Eighteenth Century, and author of a forthcoming book, *Graces of Harmony: Alliteration, Assonance, and Consonance in Eighteenth-Century Poetry.*

BRUCE I. GRANGER, professor of English at the University of Oklahoma, is the author of *Political Satire in the American Revolution* and *Benjamin Franklin: An American Man of Letters.*

JOHN GRIFFITH, assistant professor of English at the University of Washington, has published scholarly articles on American writers ranging from William Bradford in the seventeenth century to Bernard Malamud in the twentieth.

WILLIAM L. HEDGES is professor of English and American Studies at Goucher College and author of *Washington Irving: An American Study, 1802–32.*

J. A. LEO LEMAY, professor of English at UCLA, is the author of *Men of Letters in Colonial Maryland* and of *A Calendar of American Poetry in the Colonial Newspapers and Magazines.*

DAVID L. PARKER is assistant professor of English at Brown University, and has a particular interest in the evolution of Puritan conversion theology. His article "Petrus Ramus and the Puritans: The 'Logic' of Preparationist Conversion Doctrine" appears in *Early American Literature* for Fall 1973, and he is currently revising essays on Edward Taylor and Jonathan Edwards.

CAMERON C. NICKELS, professor of English at Madison College, has edited Seba Smith's *My Thirty Years Out of the Senate* and written on nineteenth-century New England humor.

LEWIS P. SIMPSON, William A. Read Professor of English Literature and coeditor *The Southern Review,* Louisiana State University, Baton Rouge, is the author of *The Man of Letters in New England and the South* and *The Dispossessed Garden: Pastoral and History in Southern Literature.*

P. M. ZALL, professor of English at California State University, Los Angeles, edited *The Simple Cobler of Aggawam in America* and the humorous works of Francis Hopkinson in *Comical Spirit of Seventy-Six.*

Index

BF stands for Benjamin Franklin. Titles of writings are listed under the author. Franklin scholars cited in the text or notes are listed together under "Franklinists."